Influential Figures of Ancient Greece

Other books in the History Makers series:

History MAKERS

Influential Figures of Ancient Greece

By Don Nardo

LUCENT BOOKS
An imprint of Thomson Gale, a part of The Thomson Corporation

THOMSON

™

GALE

Detroit • New York • San Francisco • San Diego • New Haven, Conn.
Waterville, Maine • London • Munich

On Cover: Alexander the Great, Cleopatra, Xenophon, Sophocles

© 2005 Thomson Gale, a part of The Thomson Corporation.

Thomson and Star Logo are trademarks and Gale and Lucent Books are registered trademarks used here-in under license.

For more information, contact
Lucent Books
27500 Drake Rd.
Farmington Hills, MI 48331-3535
Or you can visit our Internet site at http://www.gale.com

LIBRARY OF CONGRESS CATALOGING-IN-PUBLICATION DATA

Nardo, Don, 1947–
   Influential figures of ancient Greece / by Don Nardo.
      p. cm. — (History makers)
   Audience: Grades 7–8.
   Includes bibliographical references and index.
   ISBN 1-59018-524-2 (hardcover : alk. paper)
   1. Greece—History—to 146 B.C.—Biography—Juvenile literature. 2. Greece—History—146 B.C.–323 A.D.—Biography—Juvenile literature. I. Title. II. Series.
   DF208.N36 2004
   920.038—dc22
                                                                     2004011059

Printed in the United States of America

Contents

FOREWORD

The literary form most often referred to as "multiple biography" was perfected in the first century A.D. by Plutarch, a perceptive and talented moralist and historian who hailed from the small town of Chaeronea in central Greece. His most famous work, *Parallel Lives*, consists of a long series of biographies of noteworthy ancient Greek and Roman statesmen and military leaders. Frequently, Plutarch compares a famous Greek to a famous Roman, pointing out similarities in personality and achievements. These expertly constructed and very readable tracts provided later historians and others, including playwrights like Shakespeare, with priceless information about prominent ancient personages and also inspired new generations of writers to tackle the multiple biography genre.

The Lucent History Makers series proudly carries on the venerable tradition handed down from Plutarch. Each volume in the series consists of a set of five to eight biographies of important and influential historical figures who were linked together by a common factor. In *Rulers of Ancient Rome*, for example, all the figures were generals, consuls, or emperors of either the Roman Republic or Empire; while the subjects of *Fighters Against American Slavery*, though they lived in different places and times, all shared the same goal, namely, the eradication of human servitude. Mindful that politicians and military leaders are not (and never have been) the only people who shape the course of history, the editors of the series have also included representatives from a wide range of endeavors, including scientists, artists, writers, philosophers, religious leaders, and sports figures.

Each book is intended to give a range of figures—some well known, others less known; some who made a great impact on history, others who made only a small impact. For instance, by making Columbus's initial voyage possible, Spain's Queen Isabella I, featured in *Women Leaders of Nations*, helped to open up the New World to exploration and exploitation by the European powers. Inarguably, therefore, she made a major contribution to a series of events that had momentous consequences for the entire world. By contrast, Catherine II, the eighteenth-century Russian queen, and Golda Meir, the modern Israeli prime minister, did not play roles of global impact; however, their policies and actions significantly influenced the historical development of both their own countries and their regional neighbors. Regardless of their relative importance in the greater historical scheme, all of the figures chronicled in the History Makers series made contributions to posterity; and their public achievements, as well as what is known about their private lives, are presented and evaluated in light of the most recent scholarship.

In addition, each volume in the series is documented and substantiated by a wide array of primary and secondary source quotations. The primary source quotes enliven the text by presenting eyewitness views of the times and culture in which each history maker lived, while the secondary source quotes, taken from the works of respected modern scholars, offer expert elaboration and/ or critical commentary. Each quote is footnoted, demonstrating to the reader exactly where biographers find their information. The footnotes also provide the reader with the means of conducting additional research. Finally, to further guide and illuminate readers, each volume in the series features photographs, two bibliographies, and a comprehensive index.

The History Makers series provides both students engaged in research and more casual readers with informative, enlightening, and entertaining overviews of individuals from a variety of circumstances, professions, and backgrounds. No doubt all of them, whether loved or hated, benevolent or cruel, constructive or destructive, will remain endlessly fascinating to each new generation seeking to identify the forces that shaped their world.

Keeping Alive the Spirit of People Long Dead

Every teacher of ancient history has had a student ask him or her for a rationale for studying about Greek men and women who died more than twenty centuries ago. In today's fast-paced, busy, technology-driven world, why take the time to learn about Homer, Pericles, Aristotle, and Cleopatra? What possible bearing or relevance do such long-dead figures have on our lives today?

Societies Are Made Up of People

There are two fundamental answers to the question of why it is important and enlightening to learn about the people of ancient Greece. First, it provides people today with a better understanding of themselves and the reasons they do what they do. Western (European-based) civilization would not exist in its present form without the cultural heritage of the Greeks. The influences of their language, literature, architecture, sculpture, political ideas, social and military customs, and philosophic and scientific ideas permeate modern society, although most people remain blissfully unaware of it. Democracy, politics, trial by jury, civil liberties, the Olympics, the theater, plays, novels, history books, gymnasiums, the alphabet—all of these and more were invented or refined by the Greeks. Even the basic intellectual approach to life and learning common today in the West comes from the Greeks. In the words of one modern classical scholar:

> The Greeks provided the chromosomes of Western civilization. . . . Greek ways of exploring the cosmos, defining the problems of knowledge (and what is meant by knowledge itself), creating the language in which such problems are explored, representing the physical world and human society in the arts, [and] defining the nature of value . . . still underlie the Western cultural tradition. In some areas, the creation of mathematics, for instance, the legacy has become a universal one. All mathematicians everywhere work within a framework whose foundations are Greek.[1]

It is important, therefore, for the educated person to learn about the Greeks because what they did and thought long ago still affects what people do and think today.

Yet even if one concedes that learning about the contributions of ancient Greek civilization is fundamental, is it necessary to take the time and effort to single out individual Greeks? The answer to this question is a resounding *yes*. As is true in all societies in all ages, the Greek achievement was driven by the energy, ideas, and efforts of individuals. As historian Robert B. Kebric, author of a noted book on ancient Greek people, puts it:

> *People* make up societies, comprise civilizations. We may formulate and embrace as many theories and compile as many timetables or lists of significant events as we wish to help us understand the past, but we must always return to the simple reality that people are the foundation of our

The temple-studded Acropolis at Athens as it likely appeared during Greece's Classical Age, the period in which Pericles, Thucydides, and Plato lived.

inquiries. So often in studies of eras before our own, people have been forced into the background, assigned a role secondary to theories and events. Their humanness has been forgotten. We tend to race over their names—especially if they sound or appear foreign—to discover what happened. Who they were as individuals within the context of their times has mostly gone unnoticed.[2]

Thus, the second reason for examining the lives and contributions of Homer, Pericles, and other pivotal ancient Greek figures is that their individual ideas and energies live on within the fabric of our own lives.

Measuring the Generations

Even when a teacher convinces a student of the importance of looking back at Homer and other Greek figures, that student faces the inevitable stumbling block of placing those ancient personages in an understandable historical context. Lists of dates from any era can seem sterile and confusing, and societies and figures that existed thousands of years ago often appear impossibly distant and out of touch.

One way to make the eras in which the ancient Greeks lived more intelligible and relevant is to think about them in terms of generations. These are the familiar time spans that separate young persons from their parents, grandparents, and so forth. If one measures the passage of a human generation as twenty-five years (only one of several ways to measure it), each century witnesses the birth and interaction of four new generations.

The earliest Greeks examined in this volume—the poets Homer and Hesiod—lived in an era of ancient Greece that modern scholars call the Archaic Age, which lasted from about 800 to 500 B.C. Homer and Hesiod flourished perhaps about 700 B.C. That was about twenty-seven centuries, or about 108 generations, ago. At the time, Greece had recently emerged from a long cultural dark age in which poverty and illiteracy had been common. In the Archaic Age the Greeks saw the steady return of prosperity and the development of writing, literature (including Homer's great epic poems), arts, large-scale architecture, and major athletic games (notably the Olympic Games).

The next four figures considered—Themistocles, Pericles, Sophocles, and Euripides—lived about nine or ten generations later, in the early years of what scholars refer to as the Classical Age (ca. 500–323 B.C.). In that era, the Greeks (in large part due

10

Ancient Greece

to Themistocles' efforts) defeated invading armies of the vast Persian Empire. And the city-state of Athens initiated the world's first democracy (which Pericles championed and refined), erected the Parthenon and other famous monuments, and produced some of the greatest plays ever written (many of them by Sophocles and Euripides).

Two generations later, Athens's golden age was over. It had been defeated in a great war by its archrival, the city-state of Sparta. The historians Thucydides and Xenophon chronicled that conflict, and Xenophon went on to witness more fighting among the Greek states in the years that followed. Nonetheless, Athens was still an important cultural center and produced great thinkers such as Plato, Xenophon's contemporary, and Aristotle, a member of the following generation.

Aristotle's own contemporary, the orator Demosthenes, tried to warn all of the major Greek states about the danger posed by Philip II, king of Macedonia, in extreme northern Greece. But few listened. And with Europe's first professional standing army at his disposal, Philip defeated these states and imposed his will on them. His son, Alexander (later called "the Great"), proved even more imposing and influential. He led a Greek army into Persia and conquered that huge empire; his untimely death in 323 B.C. brought the Classical Age to a close.

In the era that followed, the Hellenistic Age (323–30 B.C.), several large and small Greek kingdoms arose in the lands Alexander had conquered. One of the most important of these was Ptolemaic Egypt, ruled by several generations of the descendants of Ptolemy I, who had been one of Alexander's generals. The Ptolemies and other Hellenistic Greek rulers, bureaucrats, artists, and thinkers brought Greek culture to other parts of the Near East as well. But the Greeks were unable to resist the military muscle of the Romans, masters of the Italian peninsula, who steadily defeated and seized control of the Greek lands. The last of the Ptolemies, Cleopatra, who lived about ten generations after Alexander and Ptolemy I, tried but failed to reverse this trend. Her death and Rome's absorption of Egypt marked the end of Hellenistic times.

Given Rome's creation of an empire encompassing the whole Mediterranean world, it is not surprising that the last ancient Greek era is called the Roman Period (30 B.C.–A.D. 476). In these years the Greeks continued to maintain and perpetuate their language, culture, and traditions. But most accepted the Roman triumph as the will of the gods, and large numbers became proud Roman citizens. One of these was the biographer Plutarch, whose writings provide invaluable information about the Greek figures who preceded him. He lived about thirty generations after Homer, about nineteen after Pericles, and about three after Cleopatra; and roughly eighty generations separate Plutarch from us. He and those he wrote about are long gone. Yet the cultural spirit that drove their lives remains alive and well in Western society. There it will continue to guide the thoughts and deeds of new generations of influential figures, as well as ordinary individuals, for as long as people have the wisdom to read about and remember their own past.

CHAPTER 1

Homer and Hesiod Define the Ancient Gods and Heroes

The Greeks who established the world's first democracies, erected the magnificent Parthenon, and conquered the vast Persian Empire looked back with pride on a rich tradition of very ancient myths. These stories were populated by heroes, villains, monsters, and gods who interacted in a legendary era the Greeks commonly referred to as the "Age of Heroes." Today, scholars know that this was actually the late Greek Bronze Age, which lasted from about 1500 to 1100 B.C. At the end of this period, the prosperous kingdoms that had long dominated the Greek mainland and Aegean islands rapidly declined and disappeared, and folk memories of these societies grew into myths in the long Dark Age (ca. 1100–800 B.C.) that followed. Among the major characters in these myths were the strongman Heracles (the Roman Hercules), who performed twelve seemingly impossible labors; the Athenian warrior Theseus, who slew a monster half-man and half-bull; Agamemnon, the king who led the Greek expedition against Troy; and numerous others. Many later Greeks believed, or at least hoped, that some of these mythical people had been real. But they could never be sure.

Later Greeks were much more certain that Homer and Hesiod were real. The two lived in a period that seemed remote to the classical Greeks—just after the end of the Dark Age. And by the opening of the Classical Age (ca. 500 B.C.), almost nothing was known about the lives of these epic poets. Yet their writings had survived and seemed to be undeniable proof that they had been real people rather than mythical characters. These writings, especially Homer's monumental epics, the *Iliad* and the *Odyssey*, came to be seen as the founding documents of Greek literature. People also saw them as crucial sources of information about the Greek gods and bottomless founts of moral instruction and practical wisdom. As the great modern scholar and translator of Homer's works Richmond Lattimore puts it, "Homer, for the Greeks, stood at the head of their literary tradition. All knew him, [and] few challenged his greatness. Hesiod . . . was sometimes thought of as his contemporary and his equal [although] Hesiod was far less widely quoted."[3] By virtue of the reverence all later Greeks had for their works, Homer and Hesiod were the earliest highly influential figures to emerge in the new and lasting Greek civilization that arose following the Dark Age.

Homer and the Oral-Epic Tradition

In fact, it is possible that Homer came into the world in the last years of the Dark Age, although exactly when and where he grew up will probably never be known. He may have been born as early as 850 B.C. or as late as 725 B.C.; most modern scholars favor a date of about 775 B.C. (based on analyses of the wording and style of his works). As for his birthplace, a number of conflicting traditions arose in ancient times, with several different Greek cities claiming to be his native town. There has been agreement among both classical Greek scholars and modern ones, however, that Smyrna and Chios (both on the Aegean coast in western Asia Minor, what is now Turkey) are the most likely candidates.

A bust of Homer, who composed the Iliad *and the* Odyssey.

Although nothing substantive or specific is known about Homer's life (ancient reports of his blindness cannot be confirmed), one thing seems almost certain. Namely, he carried on a long tradition of reciting and embellishing stories that were passed along orally from generation to generation during the Dark Age. Roving minstrels or bards, known as *aoidoi*, memorized tales about the figures and events of the Age of Heroes and performed them in meeting halls and town squares. At first, there were probably hundreds of short tales, each recalling the exploits of one or two heroes or gods. But over time, those stories that were related were combined into longer ones, and each generation of bards expanded and refined them. It is likely that this is the way lengthy epics like the *Iliad* were created.

It could well be that Homer's contribution was the most significant in this regard partly because he possessed enormous talent. But an equally important factor has to be that the Greeks rediscovered the art of writing during his lifetime. (They had slipped into illiteracy during the Dark Age.) And committing Homer's epics to paper would have allowed for the addition of more complex detail and imagery than was customarily transmitted by oral means. It is by no means certain, however, when these works were written down, which has stimulated a number of theories by scholars. Noted historian Sarah B. Pomeroy summarizes them:

> On the question of when the Homeric poems were committed to writing, and thus fossilized, so to speak, the prevailing view today is that they were written down very near the time of their composition. [Some scholars have] argued that the illiterate Homer dictated his epics to persons who could write. Other scholars, however, believe that the poems as we have them were memorized and transmitted orally by professional reciters . . . for some generations before they were written down, perhaps as late as the sixth century [the 500s B.C.]. Still others maintain that Homer was trained in the oral tradition but had learned to write, and was therefore a writing poet. Whatever the actual role of writing in the final composition of the two great epics, it is agreed that they represent the culmination of a very long oral-epic tradition, which ceased to evolve with the advent of writing.[4]

The Homeric Epics

More importantly, the *Iliad* and *Odyssey* were also the culmination of the art of epic poetry and storytelling. The title of the more-than-fifteen-thousand-line *Iliad* comes from Ilium (or Ilion), alternate names for Troy, a prominent trading city in northwestern Asia Minor that legend claimed the Greeks besieged and sacked in the later years of the Age of Heroes. The story is set in the tenth year of the war. Achilles, greatest of the Greek warriors,

Pictured is noted scholar-illustrator Peter Conolly's watercolor reconstruction of the citadel of Troy in the late Bronze Age.

suddenly quarrels with his colleague Agamemnon, leader of the Greek forces. Retiring to his tent, Achilles refuses to come out, and this demoralizes the Greek troops so much that they suffer a series of defeats at the hands of the Trojans. Only when Achilles' closest friend, Patroclus, is slain by the Trojan prince Hector does Achilles settle his differences with Agamemnon and reenter the fray. In a furious one-on-one battle, Achilles kills Hector. And the *Iliad* ends with the Greeks holding funeral games in honor of Patroclus and the Trojans doing the same for Hector.

The twelve-thousand-line *Odyssey* tells about the adventures of one of the Greek kings who led the Trojan expedition—Odysseus, king of Ithaca (an island off Greece's western coast). At the end of the war, he and his men visit the land of the Lotus-eaters, eaters of a fruit that makes them lazy and forgetful. Odysseus has to drag his men away to keep them from staying there in a stupor forever. After that, more adventures follow, including a frightening encounter with a Cyclops (one-eyed giant) on an island inhabited by a race of these creatures. The Cyclops kills and eats several of Odysseus's men, but he and the rest manage to escape. After subsequent run-ins with cannibals, a sorceress, and spirits from the Underworld, among other horrors, Odysseus loses the rest of his party and after ten long years makes it back to his native island. There, he has to fight and kill more than a hundred men who, assuming he is dead, have been vying with one another for his wife and palace. In the end, Odysseus and his wife and son are reunited.

Homer's Profound Influence

Greeks of later generations became intimately familiar with the plots and characters of these stories. And the Homeric epics exerted a pervasive and profound influence on Greek (and Roman) culture and thought for the rest of antiquity (ancient times). First, they transmitted the heroic and mythical traditions of past ages to the later Greeks. This allowed them to see the totality of these stories as a cultural heritage to be proud of and perpetuate. Men often tried to live their lives according to the moral codes of the ancient past, and many people erected shrines in honor of the long-dead heroes, believing that the spirits of these great figures might protect them.

Second, in Homer's day ancient Greek religion was still crystallizing out the combined beliefs of the Bronze and Dark ages, and his detailed descriptions of the gods helped to shape the way later Greeks viewed these deities. "The gods of Homer are mainly immortal men and women," says Lattimore, "incomparably more powerful than mortals, but like mortals susceptible to all human

In a famous scene from the Odyssey, *the giant Cyclops Polyphemus hurls boulders at the escaping Greeks.*

emotions and appetites, therefore capable of being teased, flattered, enraged, seduced, chastised."[5]

Homer's epics also served as a culturally unifying force for Greeks everywhere. Among the Greek city-states, which saw themselves as separate nations and often fought one another, the epics were seen as the common property of all Greeks and a reminder that they once stood together against a common enemy. In the words of John A. Scott, a leading Homeric scholar:

> Homer was the greatest single force in making the Greeks a kindred people and in giving them a mutually understandable language and common ideals. . . . With Homer Greek culture began, with him it flourished, with him it won dominion, [and] with him it fell. . . . No other great people has been so much the creation of a single person, and he was to the Greeks their law-giver, teacher, and poet, combining in himself the characters of Moses, David, and the prophets.[6]

Hesiod the Farmer

Although the Greeks did not place Hesiod on as high a pedestal as they did Homer, Hesiod was widely revered for his own large-scale works in poetic form. Hesiod was also a contemporary of Homer, although Hesiod was likely a child when Homer was an old man and it is not likely that the two ever met. In addition to the difference in their ages, Homer probably lived out most or all of his life in Asia Minor, whereas Hesiod was born and dwelled in Boeotia (the region lying north of Athens on the Greek mainland).

The bulk of what little information survives about Hesiod's character and life comes directly from fleeting references he made to himself in his works. In a passage from his *Theogony*, for example, he claims that as a young man the divine Muses (minor goddesses of music, literature, and other arts) appeared to him while he was tending his sheep. Supposedly they endowed him with the gift of song (i.e., poetic expression).

A passage in another writing by Hesiod, the *Works and Days*, tells how, after the death of his father, the family estate was divided between Hesiod and his brother, Perses. Perses tried to take more than his fair share, however, which ignited a bitter legal dispute. In the same work, Hesiod calls on Perses to end the feud between them and then tells several myths, the morals of which he feels illustrate the importance of justice and hard work. "O Perses," Hesiod writes,

This bust of Hesiod was fashioned centuries after he lived. No one knows what he actually looked like.

control your pride. For pride is evil in a common man. . . .
It weighs him down and leads him to disgrace. The road
to justice is the better way, for justice in the end will win
the race and pride will lose. The simpleton must learn this
fact through suffering.[7]

In the last two-thirds of the *Works and Days*, Hesiod offers his
errant brother advice on how to be a successful farmer, as well as
how to be a good citizen. The hardworking Hesiod tells how to
make a plow and how to sell one's farm products at market.
He also gives practical advice, including an almanac listing
which days are lucky and which are unlucky for planting and

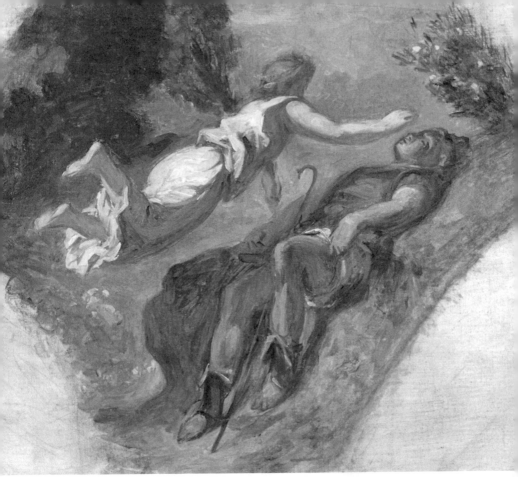

In this fanciful sketch, one of the Muses endows the sleeping Hesiod with the gift of song.

other activities. Many Greeks in later generations took to heart and followed Hesiod's advice about the proper running of a farm.

Hesiod the Mythmaker

The *Works and Days* also contains descriptions of and anecdotes about the Greek gods. One tale recounts how the early god Prometheus tricked Zeus, leader of the Olympian gods (those who were thought to dwell atop Mount Olympus, in northern Greece), by stealing fire and giving it to humans. In another passage, Hesiod tells how Zeus created Pandora, the first woman, who unleashed disease and troubles on humanity. Hesiod also recalls how the gods created various races of humans in the past, all of them better than the people living in Hesiod's time.

Hesiod's other major work, the *Theogony*, goes into even greater detail about the gods. (In fact, the word *theogony* means "the family lineage of the gods.") At the dawn of creation, Hesiod says, there was Chaos, from which emerged the gods (or natural forces) Gaia, Tartarus, and Eros. Gaia gave birth to Uranus (the Sky), and these two married and gave rise to the Titans, the earliest race of Greek gods. Hesiod goes on to explain how the Titans battled Zeus and his Olympians for control of the universe and how the Olympians prevailed.

These stories about the gods, like those about gods and heroes by Homer, exerted a powerful influence on Greeks in succeeding generations. Hesiod and Homer helped the classical Greeks to understand what the gods were like and what these divinities expected of human beings. Also, later Greek writers, including the great Athenian playwrights, frequently drew on this material for plots and characters. These later Greeks were well aware of the tremendous cultural debt they owed Homer and Hesiod, as evidenced by this famous passage by the fifth-century B.C. Athenian historian Herodotus:

> It was only . . . the day before yesterday that the Greeks came to know the origin and form of the various gods . . . for Homer and Hesiod are the poets who . . . described the gods for us, giving them all their appropriate titles, offices, and powers.[8]

CHAPTER 2

Themistocles and Pericles Lead Athens to Greatness

The fifth century B.C., roughly encompassing the first half of the Classical Age, was one of the most turbulent and momentous eras in Greece's history, as well as in the larger arena of world history. The mighty Persian Empire, centered in what are now Iran and Iraq, invaded Greece as a preliminary step in the conquest of Europe. The Greeks repelled the invaders in a series of epic battles. Then Athens rapidly built up a maritime empire stretching across the eastern Mediterranean and at the same time created a cultural outburst of democracy, art, architecture, and drama that has awed the world ever since.

The pivotal figures in Athens's ascendancy in these years were the Athenian statesmen Themistocles and Pericles. It was the politically and militarily shrewd Themistocles who convinced the Athenians that their future lay in naval power. The ships he ordered built and later commanded defeated the Persians, saved Greece from conquest, and became the chief instruments of the maritime empire Athens created after the war. Moreover, Themistocles championed and skillfully used the new democratic institutions Athens had put in place in his youth. As his modern biographer A.J. Podlecki says, "The full blossoming of Athenian democracy, when it came, was possible only because Themistocles had planted the seeds."[9]

It was Pericles who fertilized, nurtured, and raised up what grew from these seeds. A brilliant orator, politician, and general, Pericles greatly expanded Athens's influence in Greek affairs. He also initiated and personally oversaw the massive building programs that raised the Parthenon and transformed the city into a marvel of architectural splendor. With remarkable foresight, moreover, he recognized the lasting significance of these achievements. "Future ages will wonder at us," he correctly predicted, "as the present age wonders at us now."[10]

Themistocles and Pericles were unable to maintain their positions of power, esteem, and clout, however. Both men were forceful and aggressive overachievers, as Athens itself was in Greek affairs. And as history has demonstrated repeatedly, the meteoric rise of leaders and nations is almost always followed by disillusionment and decline. Despite their considerable accomplishments and influence, in the end Themistocles and Pericles each saw his policies undermined and suffered an unhappy end.

An Ambitious Young Man

Unfortunately for modern historians, Themistocles' beginning was not as well documented as his end. This is mainly because, as his ancient biographer Plutarch said, his family "was too obscure to have lent him any distinction at the beginning of his career."[11] Best

This preserved bust of the politician and naval commander Themistocles now rests in the Vatican Museum.

modern estimates place Themistocles' birth at about 523 B.C. in a village northeast of Athens.

According to Plutarch, even as a boy Themistocles knew he wanted to go into politics. "He was impetuous," Plutarch wrote,

> clever, and strongly drawn to a life of action and public service. Whenever he . . . had time to spare from his lessons, he did not play or idle like the other boys [and] was always to be found composing or rehearsing speeches by himself . . . so that [a teacher] remarked to him: "There will be nothing petty about you, my boy. You are going to be a great man one way or the other." [12]

Themistocles began to realize his political ambitions when he was elected to the office of archon in 493 B.C. In the Athenian democracy, nine elected archons acted as administrators who carried out the domestic policies of the citizen Assembly. There were also ten elected generals who enacted foreign policy, led the army, and proposed new legislation, both domestic and foreign. It appears likely that the people first voted Themistocles to one of the generalships in 490 B.C.

As archon and later as general, Themistocles strongly urged that Athens become a major naval power and advised turning the harbor of Piraeus, about five miles west of Athens's urban center,

Themistocles' ships grapple with Persian vessels in the battle of Salamis in this modern painting.

into a fortified port. His exact motivations at this time are unclear. But it is probable that he was worried that the Persians might cross the Aegean and attack the Greek mainland. (Only about a year before he became archon, a Persian fleet crushed the combined navies of the major Greek cities of Asia Minor.) This worry turned out to be well founded. In the summer of 490 B.C. the Persians came ashore at Marathon, northeast of Athens. Themistocles was one of the commanders of the Athenian army that defeated the invaders and forced them to retreat back to Asia Minor.

Victory at Salamis

Most leading Athenians and other Greeks rejoiced, assuming that Greece had seen the last of the Persians. The far-thinking Themistocles was not convinced of this, however. "He believed that [the attack at Marathon] was only the prelude to a far greater struggle," Plutarch wrote, "and he prepared . . . [to] put his city into training to meet it." [13] To that end, in the 480s B.C. Themistocles persuaded his fellow countrymen to build a fleet of warships. He also pushed through the completion of the fortifications at Piraeus. In these ways, Plutarch said, "he continued to draw the Athenians little by little and to turn their thoughts in the direction of the sea." [14]

It was not long before Themistocles' prediction—that the Persians would return—proved right. In the spring of 480 B.C. Persia's king, Xerxes (ZERK-seez), marched on Greece at the head of the largest military forces ever assembled in ancient times—some two hundred thousand combat infantry and eight hundred to one thousand ships. Fear swept through Greece, partly because the armies of the city-states were very small. But Themistocles argued that this factor would not be decisive. The wise use of sea power was the key to victory, he insisted.

Once more, Themistocles' political and military wisdom was proven right. On or about September 17, 480 B.C., the onrushing Persians entered Athens and to their surprise found it largely deserted. Themistocles had evacuated the city to keep the citizenry safe while he and the other Greek admirals prepared to meet the immense Persian fleet. The great battle took place about three days later in the Salamis strait, just north of Piraeus. Exactly as Themistocles (whose plan the Greeks followed) had foreseen, the greater Persian numbers proved to be a disadvantage in the narrow waterway; hemmed in and bunched up, the Persian ships became easy prey for the Greeks, who moved in for the kill. The

Athenian playwright Aeschylus, who fought in the battle, later wrote: "Charge followed charge on every side. . . . [The Persian] vessels heeled over; the sea was hidden, carpeted with wrecks and dead men; all the shores and reefs were full of dead."[15]

Exile and Disgrace

The Greeks followed up their tremendous victory at Salamis by smashing the Persian land army at Plataea, north of Athens, in 479 B.C. Even though the threat from Asia was over, Themistocles recognized that Athens had another enemy to worry about, one much closer to home. The politically conservative city-state of Sparta had both the most feared land army in Greece and a deep distrust of Athens and its open democracy. Athens and Sparta had emerged from the Persian wars as the leading states of Greece, and each wanted to dominate Greek affairs. Driven by this reality, Themistocles acted quickly to beef up Athenian defenses against possible Spartan aggression.

However, some leading Athenians thought it was better to work with, rather than against, the Spartans, and the pro-Spartan faction in Athens steadily grew stronger and more opposed to Themistocles' policies. In about 471 B.C. they managed to get Themistocles ostracized. Ostracism was an Athenian democratic practice similar to modern impeachment. Citizens wrote the name of a leader they wanted removed from office on broken pieces of pottery called *ostraka*, and if the person received six thousand or more of

A surviving ostrakon *from Themistocles' ostracism lists his name (at top), followed by the name of his city ward, Phrearrhios.*

these negative votes the city banished him for a period of ten years.

Exiled from his native city, Themistocles traveled from one Greek state to another, all the while continuing to speak out against Sparta. In retaliation, the Spartans accused him of collaborating with the Persians, a charge that is almost certainly false. Unfortunately for Themistocles, many of his own countrymen believed it, and the Athenian government declared him a traitor. Eventually, he reluctantly turned for refuge to the very nation he had been accused of helping—Persia. For reasons that are unclear, King Artaxerxes, Xerxes' son, allowed him to live in Asia Minor. And there Themistocles died in disgrace (in Greek eyes) in 463 B.C., at about the age of sixty.

The victory of Themistocles' political enemies over him ultimately proved to be a hollow one. As time went on, most Athenians discovered that his advocacy of naval power and anti-Spartan policies had been justified. And they came to realize his major role in Athens's rise to power. In the late fifth century B.C., the Athenian historian Thucydides said that Themistocles had exhibited "signs of genius." He had been "the best prophet of the future, even to its most distant possibilities," an "extraordinary man" who had "surpassed all others" in "meeting an emergency."[16]

The Rise of Pericles

In some ways, Themistocles' impressive legacy became clearer when his most illustrious successor in Athenian politics—Pericles— ended up following many of the same policies. On the one hand, Pericles continued the maritime expansion and democratic revolution begun by Themistocles and others. On the other, Pericles became the chief antagonist of Sparta and its allies. A dynamic and talented individual, he did everything in his power to make Athens the strongest, most influential, and most culturally splendid of the Greek states.

Pericles was born about 495 B.C., two years before Themistocles was elected archon. Very little is known about Pericles' early years, as he seems to have purposely kept a low public profile. According to Plutarch, this was in large part because he bore a striking resemblance to a former hated Athenian tyrant. Also, Plutarch recorded, Pericles' head "was rather long and out of proportion. For this reason almost all his portraits show him wearing a helmet, since the artists apparently did not wish to taunt him with this deformity."[17]

Eventually, though, Pericles did decide to get involved in politics. In the late 460s B.C., he acted as chief assistant to Ephialtes,

Pericles always wears a helmet in his busts. Rumors claimed he was self-conscious about his oddly shaped head.

the city's most liberal democratic leader. They opposed the pro-Spartan, pro-aristocratic, and generally old-fashioned politics of the conservatives, led by the popular statesman-general Cimon. Luckily for the liberals, Cimon was ostracized in 461 B.C. But unluckily for them, that same year Ephialtes was assassinated. With Cimon and Ephialtes suddenly gone, Pericles, who had first been elected general in about 465 B.C., stepped in to the vacuum; he remained the most popular Athenian leader for the next three decades. Pericles maintained this status because, as noted scholar Michael Grant points out:

He held repeated generalships, and, in spite of sharing them with nine colleagues, it was he who decided policy more often than not. . . . This was, nevertheless, free democracy in action, since Pericles . . . remained in his supreme position through a constant series of electoral votes. The Greeks were abnormally susceptible to oratory, and the oratorical talents of Pericles must have persuaded the Assembly with remarkable effectiveness and frequency.[18]

Appeals to Athenian Patriotism

Another thing that endeared Pericles to so many Athenians was that he championed the common people and the democratic institutions that endowed them with so much power. He passed a bill providing pay for jurors, which made it possible for poorer people to take time away from their work to serve the state. He also eliminated rules that allowed only those who met certain financial qualifications to hold high office.

In addition, Pericles put thousands of jobless Athenians to work on huge public building projects that often lasted for many years. The biggest of these was the transformation of the Acropolis into a magnificent complex of temples, including the Parthenon, in the 440s and 430s B.C. This made Athens the showcase of Greece and brought the Athenians much prestige and pride. It was time for Athens to realize its enormous potential, Pericles told his countrymen. "You must yourselves realize the power of Athens," he said, "and feast your eyes upon her from day to day, till love of her fills your hearts." [19]

Pericles' ability to appeal to Athenian patriotism also expressed itself in his anti-Spartan policies. He convinced the people that, to withstand a Spartan invasion and siege, landlocked Athens needed

A nineteenth-century German painting depicts Pericles delivering his great funeral oration over Athens's war dead.

a way to tap into its naval lifeline at Piraeus. The result was the Long Walls, a safe-access corridor stretching from the urban center to the sea, which permitted a virtually unlimited flow of food and other supplies during an emergency.

The construction of the Long Walls angered the Spartans, who continued to threaten Athens and did what they could to discredit Pericles. There were certainly reasons for other Greeks to dislike him. Athens collected money from the Greek city-states in its maritime empire supposedly for their mutual protection, but Pericles diverted some of the funds to pay for beautifying Athens. He also dealt harshly with Greek states that wanted to become independent of Athenian control.

Eventually, the energy, ambitions, and heavy-handedness of Periclean Athens pushed other Greeks over the edge. The Peloponnesian War erupted in 431 B.C., pitting Sparta and its allies against Athens and its own. The Athenians soon became disillusioned with Pericles' strategy, which was to allow the enemy to pillage Athens's farms while the Athenians hid behind the Long Walls. In 430, a deadly plague broke out in the crowded conditions behind the walls. Pericles himself was infected and died the following year at about the age of sixty-six.

Despite his mistakes, including getting Athens into a disastrous war, Pericles was remembered by his countrymen and by later Greeks as one of the most accomplished and influential figures Greece had ever known. Long after the war ended and faded from the public consciousness, the monuments Pericles had raised on the Acropolis remained a lasting testimonial to his leadership. This accomplishment, Plutarch later asserted,

> was one measure above all which at once gave the greatest pleasure to the Athenians, adorned their city and created amazement among the rest of mankind, and which is today the sole testimony that the tales of the ancient power and glory of Greece are no mere fables.[20]

CHAPTER 3

Sophocles and Euripides Create Drama for the Ages

During the cultural golden age that occurred in Athens in the fifth century B.C., a gifted group of artists, architects, writers, and thinkers produced works and ideas that would heavily influence all later generations in the West. Of these figures, Athenian playwrights loomed large, in both their own and later times. This is partly because Athens invented the theater and the world's first and most formative age of drama took place there. Two of the greatest dramatists of that era, Sophocles and Euripides, helped to create theatrical conventions that still underlie the fabric of Western stage, film, and television presentations.

Sophocles, Euripides, and their fellow fifth-century B.C. dramatists did not operate in a vacuum, however. The basic venue of the theater had been pieced together by a handful of Athenian innovators in the three generations that had preceded them. As near as modern scholars can tell, the theater grew out of elaborate rituals associated with worship of the fertility god Dionysus. These rituals included a kind of ceremony and verse called the dithyramb. The worshippers sang and danced to verses that told the story of Dionysus's life and exploits and eventually those of other important deities, as well as a few human heroes. These presentations increasingly took on dramatic form, as the priest, his assistants, and perhaps a selected group of worshippers in a sense acted out the stories in front of the rest of the worshippers.

Another important source for drama was epic poetry, especially Homer's *Iliad* and *Odyssey*. Traveling bards had long entertained audiences by reciting these tales. The important turning point came in 566 B.C. when the Athenians instituted Homeric recitation contests called the *rhapsodia*. These contests came together with the theatrical portions of the Dionysian rituals in about 534 B.C., when Athens initiated a large-scale annual religious festival—the

This statue of Sophocles is a later Roman marble copy of the original bronze version created in Athens circa 340 B.C.

City Dionysia—dedicated to Dionysus. The winner of the festival's first dramatic contests was a poet named Thespis. He and a handful of his contemporaries are credited with turning out the first actual scripted plays, each of which featured an actor playing two or three characters and donning a series of masks to differentiate one character from another.

Early Exposure to the Theater

By the time of Sophocles' birth, about three decades later, therefore, the theater was well established in Athens, yet still in its formative stages, with plenty of room left for experimentation and innovation. Sophocles was born in 497 or 496 B.C. at Colonus, then a village situated about a mile north of the Athenian Acropolis. Sophocles' father, Sophillus, seems to have been a well-to-do weapons maker and a leading citizen of the village.

At the time, upper-class Athenian boys received excellent educations, partly because society expected them eventually to assume leading roles in government. So Sophocles was well educated. One ancient synopsis of his life claims that he studied music under Lampros, the most distinguished musician of his time. The boy did so well in school that he won prizes in student competitions, not only in music but also in wrestling. Evidence also exists that he studied drama under Aeschylus, the world's first great playwright and by far the most dominant figure in Greek theater in the first few decades of the fifth century B.C. It is quite possible that Sophocles appeared on stage in some of Aeschylus's plays.

Therefore, Sophocles found himself from an early age at the epicenter of the societal niche in which the arts of theater and drama were rapidly evolving. He witnessed Aeschylus and other talented playwrights introducing new ideas and innovations on a regular basis. One of these was the use of a second actor. Up to that time, a lone actor had portrayed two or more characters, differentiating them by repeatedly changing masks. The dialogue was between the actor and the chorus, a group of actors who stood together as a unit on stage. Adding a second actor greatly expanded the scope of the stories writers could present because it allowed them to depict twice as many characters. The potential of this innovation was not lost on Sophocles, who as a young man was likely already contemplating the notion of a third actor. Aeschylus also introduced the trilogy, a series of three plays related in plot and theme. The trilogy, which Sophocles would later use to great effect, allowed a playwright a much larger canvas on which to paint his story.

Controversy and Innovation

In time, acting in plays and watching Aeschylus and other playwrights work must have inspired Sophocles to begin composing his own plays. No one knows when he wrote and produced his first play, but several ancient sources say that he won his first victory in the City Dionysia in 468 B.C., when he was about twenty-eight. The winning play was titled *Triptolemus*. Only a few fragments of it have survived. But it must have told the story of the mythical Athenian prince Triptolemus, whom the goddess Demeter sent to teach his fellow humans how to cultivate grain.

According to Plutarch, the play's premiere was controversial because Sophocles' supporters and those of Aeschylus got into a heated argument over whose play was better. This motivated the administrator of the dramatic contests to call on the popular politician and general Cimon to choose the winner. The administrator "noticed that the spirit of rivalry and partisanship was running

Wearing masks in the tradition of ancient Greek theater, a group of modern actors performs one of Sophocles' Oedipus plays.

high among the audience," Plutarch wrote,

> and decided not to appoint the judges of the contest by lot [random drawing], as was usually done. Instead, when Cimon and his fellow-generals entered the theater . . . he did not allow them to leave, but obliged them to take the oath and sit as judges. . . . In consequence, the fact that the judges were so distinguished raised the whole contest to a far more ambitious level. Sophocles won the prize, and it is said that Aeschylus was so distressed and indignant that he . . . [retired] in anger to Sicily.[21]

Controversy continued to follow Sophocles as he remained one of Athens's leading playwrights and introduced one theatrical innovation after another. In addition to using a third actor, which allowed for telling a more complex story, he often made the chorus participate more directly in the action. According to the later

Athenian philosopher Aristotle, Sophocles also introduced the technique of scene painting. Before, the wooden *skene*, or scene building, which rose behind the circular acting area (the orchestra), had been mostly bare, and audiences had been expected to imagine a play's setting. Decorating the immovable *skene* to represent the exterior of a palace, a temple, or some other locale added color and a touch of realism to the presentation.

Master of Character Development

Sophocles' hallmark, however, was character development, of which he became the world's first great master. "His language is more down to earth than Aeschylus's," Charles Freeman points out,

> and his characters more human and well defined as a result. One can know them as rounded individuals. . . . Sophocles is more aware of how human beings are trapped by fate, though it is often their own personalities that make the ensuing tragedy all the more unavoidable.[22]

A scene from a modern production of Sophocles' great play Oedipus the King, *performed in the Colosseum in Rome.*

Perhaps the greatest—and certainly the most memorable—character Sophocles dramatized was Oedipus, the leading figure in *Oedipus the King*. This morbid but compelling story of a man who unknowingly murders his father and then marries his mother is frequently seen by critics and scholars as the greatest tragedy ever written.

The immense literary and social influence of this single play begs the question of what Sophocles' impact might have been had all of his works survived. The sad fact is that, of the 123 plays attributed to him by ancient sources, only seven have survived completely intact. Besides *Oedipus the King* (429 B.C.), these are *Ajax* (447); *Antigone* (441); *The Women of Trachis* (ca. 428); *Electra* (ca. 415); *Philoctetes* (409); and *Oedipus at Colonus* (406). Many of the lost plays must have been as great as these, since Sophocles won the City Dionysia competition no less than eighteen times, a record never equaled by another ancient playwright.

While writing and producing these and other plays, Sophocles found the time to serve his community in various public offices. In 443 B.C. Pericles appointed him chief treasurer in charge of collecting money from the member states of Athens's maritime empire. Three years later, the dramatist was elected one of Athens's ten generals, a post he served in for a year. Some evidence suggests that Sophocles was elected to another term as general in 415 B.C., when he was eighty-one.

Little else is known about Sophocles' private life and personal character. One surviving fact comes from his colleague, the comic playwright Aristophanes. In his play *Frogs*, the latter says of Sophocles: "[A] gentleman always, [he] is a gentleman still."[23] A few other brief references in ancient sources suggest that Sophocles was a gentle, caring, and pious individual. He died in 406 B.C. at the age of ninety or ninety-one.

The First "Modern" Playwright

Ancient sources suggest that Sophocles was on good terms with his younger colleague Euripides. Their dramatic approaches and styles were very different, however. While Sophocles carefully upheld traditional religious and social values in his works, Euripides frequently questioned these values. Euripides portrayed humans in a more realistic (rather than heroic) manner and often gave strong voices to characters from society's lower ranks—notably women and slaves. Sophocles was reported to have said that he himself showed people as they should be while Euripides showed people as they are.

One result of Euripides' less conventional approach to drama was that he was sometimes seen as undignified and a maverick, and so he enjoyed less popularity in his own time than Sophocles and Aeschylus did. However, today scholars view Euripides as equal in stature to Sophocles, partly because Euripides was the first playwright to deal with human problems in a modern way. As scholar Jacqueline de Romilly puts it:

> In his own time, Euripides was essentially a "modern." His studies of passion, his insistence on human weakness, and his realism are all clear indications of that modernity.

This Roman marble copy of an original Greek bronze shows Euripides holding the traditional mask of tragedy.

. . . He created new and action-filled plots. In his work we may recognize a true dramatic *technique* in the modern sense of the word.[24]

A good example of this technique is the way Euripides boldly challenged accepted societal conventions, something most of the best examples of modern drama do on a regular basis. In his play *Electra*, for instance, he points out the hollowness and unfairness of class distinctions, which were still strong in Athens despite the recent rise of democracy. The hero of the play asserts:

> There is no clear sign to tell the quality of a man. Nature and place turn vice and virtue upside down. I've seen a noble father breed a worthless son, and good sons come of

An engraving shows a scene from a production of Euripides' Alcestis, *performed in the 1800s by an all-female cast.*

evil parents; a starved soul housed in a rich man's palace, a great heart dressed in rags. By what sign, then, shall one tell good from bad? By wealth? Wealth's a false standard. By possessing nothing, then? No; poverty is a disease; and want itself trains men in crime. . . . The best way is to judge each man as you find him; there's no rule.[25]

Euripides' Surviving Plays

Considering that Euripides' work as a playwright was so well known and controversial, it is perhaps odd, and certainly unfortunate, that so little is known about his personal life. The main surviving facts are that he was born about 485 B.C. in Athens; his father's name was Mnesarchus; and his mother, Cleito, sold herbs in the marketplace, at least according to Aristophanes and other comic playwrights who poked fun at Euripides and his family. It is also recorded that Euripides had a wife named Melito and three sons. In 408 B.C. he traveled to Macedonia, likely at the invitation of the local king. And the playwright died there in 406, shortly before the passing of his older friend, Sophocles.

Making up to some degree for the shortage of evidence about Euripides' private life is the fact that many more of his plays survived the ravages of time than did those of Aeschylus, Sophocles, and Aristophanes. Of the eighty-eight to ninety plays attributed to Euripides by ancient sources, nineteen have survived complete. In order of their composition, they are as follows: *Alcestis* (438 B.C.), *Medea* (431), *Children of Heracles* (ca. 430), *Hippolytus* (428), *Andromache* (ca. 426), *Hecuba* (ca. 424), *The Suppliant Women* (ca. 422), *Madness of Heracles* (ca. 420–417), *Electra* (ca. 417–413), *The Trojan Women* (415), *Iphigenia in Taurus* (ca. 414), *The Phoenician Women* (ca. 412–408), *Helen* (412), *Ion* (ca. 412), *Orestes* (408), *The Bacchae* (405), *Iphigenia in Aulus* (ca. 405), *The Cyclops* (date unknown), and *Rhesus* (date unknown).

These and Euripides' other plays became increasingly popular after his death as audiences came to see that he had been ahead of his time in portraying emotions and realism on stage. And many of these works continue to be performed today. The most famous and riveting to both ancient and modern audiences is probably *Medea*, the story of a woman who achieves her revenge on her husband's betrayal and infidelity by killing their children. The work's lasting popularity can be attributed to the fact that its themes—failed marriage, treatment of women as second-class beings, betrayal, jealousy, deceit, revenge, and murder—are universal and often gut-wrenching to every society in every era. Like Sophocles, therefore, Euripides wrote drama not only for his own time but for the ages. And through the survival and influence of their works, a part of ancient Athenian society remains vital and meaningful for each new human generation.

CHAPTER 4

Thucydides and Xenophon Chronicle Greece's Wars

Among many other literary genres, the Greeks invented historical writing. Before the rise of the Greek historians in the fifth century B.C., writers who dealt with the past typically retold old myths. Or they wrote down official, biased versions of battles and other major events, accounts commissioned by and designed to flatter the victors.

The first known attempt to treat an event or time period as a piece of history to be reported with some semblance of accuracy and objectivity was Herodotus's *Histories*, composed in the mid–fifth century B.C. Born at Halicarnassus (in southern Asia Minor) in about 490 B.C., Herodotus set out to chronicle the Greco-Persian wars, which he saw as the greatest event of history to date. In the opening of his book, he states his purpose: "To preserve the memory of the past by putting on record the astonishing achievements both of our own and of other peoples; and more particularly, to show how they came into conflict."[26]

Herodotus's history book is a colorful and often revealing compilation of anecdotes about the peoples and events of his times. Despite its many positive attributes, however, it is often less than objective. It is also filled with hearsay, rumors, and thirdhand information and freely incorporates omens, oracles, and other supernatural elements as if they are real and meaningful.

For the first true history book in the modern sense—an unbiased account of events based on firsthand information—one must turn to Herodotus's younger contemporary, the Athenian Thucydides. He, too, chose war as his subject. In this case, it was the Peloponnesian War, which broke out in 431 B.C. and engulfed nearly all of the Greek city-states. Unlike Herodotus, Thucydides reported only those events that he or someone he interviewed had witnessed firsthand. "With regard to my factual reporting of events," Thucydides writes in the first chapter,

> I have made it a principle not to write down the first story that came my way, and not even to be guided by my own general impressions; either I was present myself at the events which I have described or else I heard of them from eye-witnesses whose reports I have checked with as much thoroughness as possible.[27]

Indeed, Thucydides was such a distinguished historian that he became the model for all historical writers who followed, although few were able to match his objectivity and narrative talents. One who tried was his own younger contemporary, the Athenian estate owner, adventurer, and historian Xenophon (ZEN-uh-phon). Though not as skilled a historian as Thucydides, Xenophon dutifully chronicled the main events of several pivotal conflicts and battles of the fourth century B.C. Among these was the immortal "March of the Ten Thousand," in which he himself took part.

Thucydides and Xenophon had much in common, therefore. Each was a warrior who became caught up in the major events of his day and captured these events for posterity. At the same time, each was the main source of information about his own life.

Clues to Thucydides' Early Years

In fact, practically all that is known about Thucydides' life comes from statements he made about himself in his book. Since he does not mention when he was born, the date is uncertain; however, most modern scholars think it was sometime between 460 and 455 B.C.,

A drawing based on a bust of Herodotus. As a historian, he was not as careful and critical as Thucydides.

The bust on which this drawing is based purportedly depicts Thucydides.

shortly after Pericles' rise to power in Athens. In a short passage, Plutarch does provide some valuable information about Thucydides' family background. Thucydides' father, Olorus, was an Athenian citizen who was descended from a wealthy family from southern Thrace (bordering the Aegean's northern rim). One prominent member of the family, Plutarch says, was Cimon, Pericles' early political rival. Through his family connections, Thucydides had access to an estate in Thrace, and "he was the owner of gold mines"[28] there, Plutarch adds.

The next solid piece of information about Thucydides is that he began writing about the long, grueling Peloponnesian War shortly after it started in 431 B.C. "I lived through the whole of it," he recorded in his book, "being of age to understand what was happening, and I put my mind to the subject so as to get an accurate view of it."[29]

Not long after the outbreak of the war, Thucydides was still in Athens, for he recorded in meticulous detail the terrible plague that struck the city in the spring of 430 B.C. In fact, he himself contracted the disease and was fortunate to be one of the few infected who survived. "I had the disease myself," he writes, "and saw others suffering from it." He goes on to describe how the survivors, including himself, had a unique perspective on the disaster:

> The ones who felt most pity for the sick and the dying were those who had had the plague themselves and had recovered from it. They knew what it was like and at the same time felt themselves to be safe, for no one caught the disease twice. . . . Such people . . . were so elated at the time of their recovery that they fondly imagined that they could never die of any other disease in the future.[30]

Military Service and Exile

It was fortunate for Athens that Thucydides survived the plague because the city needed all the able-bodied men it could find to fight the Spartans and their allies. Thucydides served as one of Athens's ten generals in 424 B.C. and was charged with guarding the town of Amphipolis, Athens's main stronghold in the northern Aegean. Amphipolis was located on the coast of Thrace near Thucydides' family estate, and it seems likely that the Assembly gave him the assignment because he knew the area well.

Trouble soon erupted in Thrace, events that turned out to be the turning point of Thucydides' life. Late in 424 B.C., the Spartan general Brasidas unexpectedly moved on Amphipolis and demanded its surrender. At the time, Thucydides' seven warships were docked at the island of Thasos, about half a day's sail away. "As soon as [I] heard the news," he wrote, "[I] set sail at once. . . . [My] first aim, certainly, was to reach Amphipolis in time to prevent its surrender."[31] However, Thucydides and his men arrived too late. Brasidas seized control of the town, an event that the Athenians viewed as a major setback in the war. The Assembly punished Thucydides for his failure to prevent it by banishing him from Athens indefinitely.

The soldier-historian spent the next twenty years traveling from place to place in the Greek sphere, gathering information for his book, which grew longer and longer as the war dragged on. He may have used the family estate in Thrace as a home base. After twenty-seven arduous years, the conflict finally ended with Athens's surrender in 404 B.C. Soon afterward Thucydides was allowed to return to his native city. But he apparently did not stay there very long. He soon returned to the estate in Thrace, where he died in 400 or 399 at about the age of sixty.

According to Plutarch, Thucydides was murdered, although he does not say who did it and why. Most scholars think this scenario was based on hearsay and is not wholly credible. But it does satisfactorily explain why Thucydides' great historical work breaks off in mid-sentence in a passage describing events in 411 B.C., seven years before the war's conclusion.

The Young and Disillusioned Xenophon

Whatever the nature of Thucydides' death, his chronicle of the great war remained incomplete. And the task of finishing it fell to other Greek historians. At least three tackled the job. But of these, Xenophon's version is the only one that has survived. Titled *Hellenica* (meaning "History of Greece"), it covers major events from

411 B.C., where Thucydides left off, to 362 B.C., the year of the pivotal battle of Mantinea. Though it was and remains an important historical tract, Xenophon's book suffers from his faults as a historian. The major ones are his frequent omission of crucial events and his lack of objectivity, as he tended to take sides and be overly critical of people he did not like.

Chronologically speaking, the *Hellenica* (at least the major portions of it) was one of Xenophon's last works and capped a long and event-filled life. He was born into a wealthy family in Athens in about 430 B.C., the year the plague struck the city and the year after the Peloponnesian War broke out. Thus, Xenophon's entire childhood and young manhood took place during a prolonged and bloody conflict, a situation that was bound to color his thinking. Indeed, like many young men of his generation, he became disillusioned with Athens's democracy. This was partly because the Assembly, driven by desperation and emotion, made some rash and in some cases shameful decisions in the war's last years. In one episode that particularly appalled Xenophon, in 406 B.C. the government unlawfully executed six of its generals for misconduct.

Xenophon shared his contempt for Athens's democracy with the philosopher Socrates, an eccentric character who wandered the streets and challenged people to reexamine their lives and views of the world. Like other followers of Socrates, Xenophon was extremely upset when the state condemned the philosopher to death in 399 B.C. on charges that were clearly trumped up. In his work titled *Memorabilia* the younger man called the execution unjust, saying that "Nobody ever saw Socrates do, or heard him say, anything" wrong and that "he deserved to be honored by the state rather than executed."[32]

The March of the Ten Thousand

Xenophon was not in Athens at the time of Socrates' death, however, and learned of his friend's execution secondhand. In 401 B.C., the young man had signed on as one of several thousand Greek mercenaries (hired soldiers) that formed part of a larger army assembled by a Persian prince named Cyrus. Cyrus's goal was to dethrone his elder brother, King Artaxerxes II. The brothers' armies had their big showdown later that year at Cunaxa, about fifty miles from Babylon (in what is now Iraq). Cyrus was defeated and killed, but the Greek contingent of his army fought with distinction and emerged almost completely intact.

Xenophon chronicled what happened next in his exciting adventure chronicle, the *Anabasis* ("March Up-Country"). Artaxerxes' officers invited the Greek leaders to a peace negotiation and then treacherously murdered them. The outraged Greek soldiers responded by choosing new leaders, the youngest among them Xenophon, who described the dire situation they were now in:

> They [the Greeks] were distant from Greece more than a thousand miles, with no guide for the road. Impassable rivers crossed the homeward way, and they had been deserted even by the natives who had come up country with Cyrus.[33]

This nineteenth-century artistic rendering of Xenophon is completely fanciful.

Undaunted, the Greek band endured incredible hardships, including almost constant attacks by Persian troops and fierce hill tribesmen. Yet the "Ten Thousand," as they became known, managed to reach the shores of the Black Sea, from which they eventually made it home. More importantly, Greeks everywhere heard about and learned from their harrowing experience. Xenophon and the others had shown that even a small, ill-supplied Greek army could fight its way through Persia and emerge in one piece; what damage, then, might a far larger and better supplied Greek force inflict on Persia? For the Greek world, the exploits of the Ten Thousand became in a sense a military manual on how to defeat the Persians.

The Country Gentleman

After the Ten Thousand made it to the Greek lands bordering the Black Sea, Xenophon decided to continue his life as a soldier of fortune. This time he signed on with the Spartans, who were fighting the Persians in Asia Minor. In 396 B.C. he met and became a close friend of the Spartan king Agesilaus. Two years later, Xenophon followed Agesilaus back to Greece and fought alongside him at the battle of

Coronea, in which Sparta faced a coalition of Greek states, including Xenophon's native Athens. Afterward, Xenophon could not go home because the Athenians had banished him (mainly for helping Cyrus earlier), so he stayed with the Spartans. Agesilaus granted him a fine estate at Scillus, near Olympia.

Thus, Xenophon settled down to the life of a country gentleman and spent the next twenty years tending his lands and writing books. One of these, the *Oeconomicus* ("Estate Manager," or "Householder"), became a popular guide for well-to-do Greek landowners. Unfortunately for Xenophon, his fortunes were largely tied to those of the Spartans, and when Thebes soundly defeated Sparta in 371 B.C., he lost his beloved estate. Sometime in the 360s he apparently returned to Athens, where his exile was lifted, but it is unclear how long he stayed there. Eventually he moved to Corinth (about sixty miles west of Athens), where he died around 354 B.C.

The Greeks making up the band called the Ten Thousand rejoice at reaching the Black Sea after their long and dangerous march through Persia.

Some of Xenophon's minor works had military themes, including On Horsemanship, *here illustrated for a modern edition.*

In the centuries that followed, Xenophon's versatility and readable narratives made him the most popular Greek prose writer among the Romans (and early modern Europeans as well). Meanwhile, the war tract of his older peer Thucydides remained essential reading for many generations to come in the West. In fact, these two writers essentially created the genre of political history. It is in large part due to them, Michael Grant points out, "that Western civilization has regarded politics as the central concern and study of the human race."[34]

CHAPTER 5

Plato and Aristotle Explore the Frontiers of Knowledge

Although Athens suffered defeat in the destructive Peloponnesian War in the last years of the fifth century B.C., it remained one of Greece's leading cities for a long time to come. It became especially renowned as an intellectual center where noted philosophers gathered and taught. In the fourth century B.C., Athens produced two of Western civilization's greatest thinkers: Plato and Aristotle. Like Xenophon, Plato was an admirer and follower of Socrates, who was executed by the Athenian government in 399 B.C. In turn, Aristotle was Plato's student.

The influence of Plato and Aristotle, in both ancient times and later ages, cannot be overstated. The noted modern English philosopher Alfred North Whitehead once quipped that the entire Western philosophical tradition has been "a series of footnotes to Plato." [35] Although exaggerated, this statement emphasizes a fact that applies to Aristotle as well. Namely, all Western thinkers since Plato and Aristotle have either adopted some or all of their ideas or at least felt obligated to explain why they disagreed with those ideas.

Plato's Formative Influences

Plato's first major accomplishment was to preserve for posterity the ideas of his mentor, Socrates, who left no writings of his own. It was Socrates who had the most important influence on the young Plato, who was born in Athens in 427 B.C., shortly after the outbreak of the Peloponnesian War. Plato's father, Ariston, and mother, Perictione, were wealthy, so the boy received a first-class education. Yet the teachings he valued most were those he acquired from Socrates, whom he seems to have met through family connections in about 407 B.C.

Plato quickly learned to appreciate Socrates' unorthodox teaching method. It consisted of urging a person to take stock of himself or herself and to seek after justice and truth. Socrates guided the conversation by asking a series of penetrating questions about a subject; the person's answers became a sort of trail leading to the discovery of the truth of that subject, at least as it related to him or her. This approach to learning eventually became known as the "Socratic method" in Socrates' honor. Plato later described how challenging one of these sessions could be:

> Anyone who . . . enters into conversation with [Socrates] is liable to be drawn into an argument; and whatever subject he may start, he will be continually carried round and round by him, until at last he finds that he has to give an account both of his present and past life; and when he is once entangled, Socrates will not let him go until he has completely and thoroughly sifted him.[36]

Socrates taught Plato to question everything about one's self and one's society, including authority figures and the government. This lesson hit home particularly hard for Plato when the Athenian state accused Socrates of corrupting the city's youth and proceeded to execute him. Realizing the charge was false, Plato was

This nineteenth-century painting shows the Athenian philosopher Socrates (at right) visiting his friend Alcibiades.

deeply disheartened and no longer felt comfortable in his native city. Shortly after the execution, he left and for the next few years traveled through Greece, Egypt, and southern Italy (where a number of Greek cities then held sway).

Plato's immediate goal in these travels was to observe the way various states governed themselves. In the long run, he hoped to devote himself, as Socrates had, to philosophy and to show his fellow Greeks how to apply philosophical ideas in a practical way. Most importantly, Plato wanted to demonstrate that rulers could and must be fair and just. He believed that philosophers could teach rulers these qualities or, better still, that the philosophers should become the rulers.

Plato's Ideal State

Today, such ideas sound idealistic, even naive. Yet in Athens and other parts of Greece in Plato's day there was an audience willing

A nineteenth-century engraving depicts Plato meeting with some of his students in the garden of the Academy.

to at least listen to such notions. There was an enormous thirst for knowledge among young men (young Greek women usually did not receive formal educations), especially those from well-to-do families. And many were eager to study with a handful of noted teachers and philosophers.

Plato soon became a member of this elite. In about 387 B.C., when he was roughly forty, he returned to Athens, bought a plot of land, and on it established the world's first university-like school for higher learning. Plato initially dedicated the school, which he called the Academy, to turning out a new breed of statesmen—potential rulers having strong moral centers and a commitment to justice. These ideas did prove to be naive, for the Academy never produced a single noble philosopher-king. Nevertheless, it prospered, survived for more than nine hundred years, and inspired the founding of thousands of other scholarly centers across the known world.

Plato spent the rest of his long life at the Academy, acting as its director and turning out numerous writings expressing his ideas about the natural world and the human condition. Most of these are in the form of dialogues, in which a group of people discuss the pros and cons of an issue. Not surprisingly, one of the major recurring themes in these writings is justice. Plato's most detailed exploration of the concept appears in his great masterwork, the *Republic*. In it, he envisions an ideal political state in which the rulers are honest, just, and constructive.

The noble ruler constitutes only one element of Plato's ideal state, however. He goes on to formulate a utopian (ideal) society that today would be called communistic. Helping the philosopher-king govern are the "guardians," superior individuals who share their property with one another. These men administer the rest of the citizens, each of whom has certain duties that must be performed without question, giving thought only to the good of the greater community. Individuality and political and cultural innovation are discouraged in the Platonic state because they might lead to disorder.

Surveying the Universe

Individualism was better expressed on a deeper level, Plato maintained, namely in the guise of the human soul. He saw the soul as perfect and immortal and the ideal form of a human, whose physical form was imperfect and transient. This idea was central to Plato's "doctrine of a material world . . . governed by something nonmaterial," Michael Grant points out.

Behind perceived phenomena [according to Plato] there is a true, eternal, unchanging reality. It is this idealistic conviction that has earned Plato his overwhelming influence on the philosophical and religious thought of the later Western world.[37]

Plato's thirst for knowledge led him to attempt to survey the whole known universe in his dialogue the *Timaeus*, which describes the formation of the cosmos and humanity's place within it. Later scientists came to see it as the founding document of cosmology, the branch of astronomy dealing with the universe's origins. The work, composed when Plato was an old man, was intended as the first third of a trilogy that would tell the entire history of the universe right up to Plato's own day. However, he failed to finish the second volume and never started the third.

Instead, he returned to the subject of the best possible society and political system in his longest single work, the *Laws*. The society envisioned in this treatise is similar to the one in the *Republic*, although somewhat less authoritarian. The *Laws* turned out to be Plato's last work, for shortly after finishing it in 347 B.C., he died at the age of eighty.

"The Mind"

Plato's ideas outlived him. And even those who disagreed with him felt his influence. A good example of this was Aristotle, who studied under Plato yet eventually developed his own distinctive views. Born in 384 B.C. at Stagira (on the northern Aegean coast), Aristotle grew up in a household where learning and intellectual pursuits were strongly encouraged. His father, Nicomachus, was a physician to Amyntas II, king of Macedonia. Unfortunately for Aristotle, Macedonia was then a culturally backward place and had no schools of higher learning; moreover, there was only so much the young man could learn from his father. So in 367 B.C., at age seventeen, Aristotle traveled to Athens and enrolled at the Academy.

During the twenty years that Aristotle spent at the school, at first as a student and later as an instructor, he got to know Plato extremely well. The older man affectionately called Aristotle "the mind" and "the reader," likely describing the younger man's remarkable ability to absorb huge amounts of information. That Aristotle held Plato in equal esteem is revealed by the fact that Aristotle's earliest written works were dialogues similar to those of his mentor.

This drawing is based on an idealized bust of Aristotle, probably from the time when he taught at Plato's Academy.

Aristotle's Travels

The relationship between the two men was evidently so strong that Plato's death in 347 B.C. marked a major turning point in Aristotle's life. Now in his midthirties, Aristotle decided it was time for him to leave Athens and establish his own school. He and a colleague, Theophrastus (who would later become known as the father of botany), at first opened a small Academy-like school in a Greek town in northwestern Asia Minor. Later, they moved to the large Greek island of Lesbos and established a school there.

During this period, Aristotle married a young woman named Pythias. The depth of his feelings for her is revealed by what happened following her premature death only a few years later. Though he went on to marry another woman (Herpyllis), who gave him a son and daughter, he later directed in his will that Pythias's remains be placed beside his in his tomb.

Aristotle (right) tutors the young Macedonian crown prince Alexander III in Pella, Macedonia's capital.

Over time Aristotle built a name for himself as a scholar. And in 343 B.C. Macedonia's King Philip II invited him to come and tutor the crown prince, Alexander III (later called "the Great"). Aristotle accepted and remained in Macedonia until 336, when Philip was assassinated and Alexander ascended the throne. Aristotle then returned to Athens, where he soon founded another school, the Lyceum.

Studies in Cosmology and Biology

During the next twelve years, all spent at the Lyceum, Aristotle produced the bulk of his most influential written works. Nearly all were published, and numerous ancient writers praised them as stylish, witty, and very readable. Most of these treatises did not survive, however. The huge collection of Aristotle's writings that did survive consists mainly of his notes, rough drafts of his lectures, and notes made at his lectures by his students. They are dry, formal tracts that can be a chore to read, even for Aristotelian enthusiasts.

Nevertheless, these works have served the vital function of conveying Aristotle's principal ideas to later generations. Some of these ideas deal with the cosmos and its structure. He agreed with Plato and other earlier Greeks that all matter was composed of four basic elements—earth, water, air, and fire. In Aristotle's view, however, these were imperfect and changeable, so they existed only on Earth. By contrast, he said, the heavens were permanent and eternal, so they consisted of a special fifth element, which he called the "ether." Aristotle also argued that Earth was a sphere floating at the center of the universe. Surrounding Earth, he asserted, were fifty-five larger spheres nested within one another, each transparent and each holding a planet or other celestial body. These views of the cosmos became so influential that they dominated the field of astronomy for nearly two thousand years.

Aristotle also explored the animal kingdom. He collected literally thousands of observations and specimens, which allowed him to launch studies in many areas of biology, including comparative anatomy, ethology (animal habits), embryology (prebirth development), and ecology (animals' relation to their environment). He

Aristotle's Heavenly Spheres

Moon   Earth   Venus   Sun   Mars

This simplified cutaway view of the celestial system proposed by Eudoxos and expanded by Aristotle shows the central Earth encased by concentric spheres, each carrying a heavenly body; the outermost sphere holds the stars.

studied more than 540 species and performed dissections on at least 50. These endeavors revealed to him that whales and dolphins are mammals like humans, that cows have four-chambered stomachs, and that birds and reptiles are anatomically similar. In addition, he devised a system of zoological classification, which neatly grouped the known animal species by type. Aristotle's studies of animals were so fundamental and far-ranging that modern scientists recognize him as the father of biology.

To Unravel Nature's Mysteries

With nearly equal vigor, Aristotle explored politics, law, logic, physics, ethics, literary criticism, and other intellectual disciplines. These endeavors were unexpectedly interrupted, however, when the news came in 323 B.C. that Alexander, who had ruled the Greek world for more than a decade, had died. Most Greeks hated Alexander and had followed him mainly out of fear, so a wave of anti-Macedonian feeling now swept through Greece. Because Aristotle had been Alexander's friend and tutor, the Athenians tried him as an enemy of the state, which forced him to flee northward to the island of Euboea. A few months later, in November 322 B.C., he died at the age of sixty-two.

Aristotle's impact on later philosophical and scientific thought was profound. As Charles Freeman puts it, "His search for a total understanding of the whole range of human experience and the nature of the physical world makes him one of the key figures, perhaps *the* key figure, in the development of the scientific tradition." Moreover, he and his mentor, Plato, established the notion that human beings can ultimately unravel the mysteries of nature and surpass the frontiers of knowledge. They demonstrated to later generations that "there is an underlying, if not immediately visible, order to life which can be grasped by the reasoning mind." [38]

CHAPTER 6

Philip and Demosthenes Clash over Greece's Freedom

In the early fourth century B.C., when Xenophon was minding his farm near Olympia and Plato was teaching the young Aristotle at the Academy, Greece was in a state of profound political transition, though few people recognized it at the time. For centuries, city-states had dominated Greek affairs. Fiercely independent, they had often taken turbulent, bloody paths. In the last quarter of the fifth century, the Peloponnesian War had devastated large sections of Greece. And failing to learn the lesson of that conflict (that disunity was futile and fatal), the city-states continued to fight one another in the following century. The result was ultimately stalemate, exhaustion, and vulnerability to attack from an unexpected quarter.

That unexpected quarter turned out to be the kingdom of Macedonia, in far northern Greece. Itself long disunited, militarily weak, and culturally backward, Macedonia had appeared in the eyes of the southern city-states to be a backwash on the fringes of their world and an unlikely source of trouble. But in about 382 B.C. a boy named Philip II was born into Macedonia's royal family. He was destined to change the fortunes of not only his native land but Greece as a whole, by challenging the dominance and independence of the city-states.

These states were not about to go down without a fight, however. About the same year that Philip came into the world, an Athenian family produced a boy named Demosthenes, who was fated to lead the resistance against Macedonia and to blacken Philip's image in the eyes of history. Perhaps nowhere else in the long saga of ancient Greece were the efforts of two figures so different in background and temperament so closely intertwined at cross-purposes.

Wisdom Beyond His Years

Philip's purpose, or goal—to impose his will on the city-states—did not become foremost in his agenda until well after he became king. He was born the youngest son of Macedonia's King Amyntas III at a time when the country was divided into "lowland" and "highland" regions that often feuded. When Philip was in his early teens, Amyntas died, leaving the eldest son, Alexander II, on the throne. Alexander was soon murdered, however, and Philip's other brother, Perdiccas III, became king. Finally, in 359 B.C., Perdiccas was killed in battle and Philip, then about twenty-two, ascended the throne of the still disunited Macedonia.

Fortunately for Philip, he possessed some qualities that his father and brothers had lacked, namely a brilliant mind, tremendous resiliency, and political and military wisdom way beyond his years. Shortly before his death, Perdiccas had put Philip in charge of the kingdom's small, largely ineffective army. This became the

This small ivory portrait, discovered in an ancient tomb at Vergina, in northern Greece, is thought to depict King Philip II.

A speira, consisting of 256 men, was the basic unit of the Macedonian phalanx. Each member carried a long battle pike.

tool with which Philip now unified the country. He created a strong centralized military organization that emphasized nationalism, patriotism, and loyalty to him and the throne. The new institution attracted young men from both the lowland and highland regions; they learned to get along with one another, train together, fight as a unit, and pursue national goals.

This professional standing army, Europe's first, which Philip honed and drilled in the 350s B.C., consisted of several different elements, each of which supported and strengthened the others. First, Philip improved the traditional Greek phalanx, a block of soldiers standing in rows, one behind the other, and wielding thrusting spears and swords. He deepened the formation's ranks and replaced the spears with long pikes. Their points projected from the front of the phalanx, forming an impenetrable, hedgehoglike mass of sharpened metal.

Another key element in Philip's new army was an elite cavalry corps of young noblemen—the "companion cavalry." Horsemen had long been used in Greek warfare, but mainly to protect the phalanx against enemy skirmishers (javelin throwers and archers) and to chase down escaping enemy troops. Philip dressed his cavalrymen in armor and trained them to charge in a wedge-shaped formation directly at enemy infantry. Though these horsemen could not defeat a phalanx on their own, under Philip's direction they softened up the enemy before the attack of the "Macedonian phalanx," as his infantry came to be known. Philip also effectively employed light-armed soldiers, including archers, slingers, and peltasts (javelin men), adding to the versatility and lethality of his army.

A Series of Bold Moves

Philip wasted little time in putting this army to the test. In 357 B.C. he captured Amphipolis, the Athenian colony that Thucydides had failed to protect during the Peloponnesian War. Athens promptly declared war on Philip. But the Athenians' bark proved worse than their bite, for they were unwilling to send troops so far from home. Their inaction allowed Philip to seize the rich gold mines located near Amphipolis. He then proceeded to seize Pydna, Potidaea, Methone, and several other northern Aegean cities. In a similar manner, Philip steadily extended his influence southward in the direction of Athens, Thebes, Corinth, and Greece's other major powers.

Philip was no mere heavy-handed military bully, however. In addition to, and often instead of, naked force, he brilliantly employed a number of other means to achieve his goals. The first-century B.C. Greek historian Diodorus Siculus wrote that Philip's success "was not due so much to his prowess in arms as to his adroitness and cordiality in diplomacy. Philip himself is said to have been prouder of his grasp of strategy and his diplomatic successes than of his valor in actual battle." [39] True, Philip's diplomacy frequently consisted of intrigues, bribery, half-truths, and outright lies. But these were often effective tools in the practical realm of Greek politics. As the noted historian J.F.C. Fuller points out, Philip was an opportunist who believed the end was justified by whatever means were necessary:

> He was recklessly brave, yet unlike so many brave generals he would at once set force aside should he consider that bribery or liberality or feigned friendship was more likely to secure his end. He possessed in marked degree the gift of divining what was in his enemy's mind and when beaten in the field would accept defeat and prepare for victory. [40]

Still another factor that worked in Philip's favor was the slowness of the major city-states to organize any resistance to his aggressions. In 346 B.C., for example, he boldly moved into southern Greece and seized the religious sanctuary at Delphi, home of the famous oracle. "The news stunned the Athenians," Plutarch wrote. "No speaker dared to mount the rostrum, nobody knew what advice should be given, [and] the Assembly was struck dumb and appeared to be completely at a loss." [41]

A New Political Order Dawns

Eventually, a hastily formed alliance of city-states, led by Athens and Thebes, did try to halt Philip's advance. They engaged him at Chaeronea, in western Boeotia, in 338 B.C., but they could match neither the power of his army nor his skills as a general. Philip led the right wing of his phalanx himself and pretended to retreat. The Athenians took the bait and launched a wild charge, which separated them from the Thebans and other allies and opened a fatal gap in the allied line. The Macedonian companion cavalry, commanded by Philip's eighteen-year-old son, Alexander III, then charged into the gap. At the same time, Philip's phalanx suddenly spun around and charged, sending most of the enemy into flight.

The showdown at Chaeronea was one of the most decisive battles in Western history. Philip's victory exposed the disunity and impotence of the city-states and signaled the dawn of a new political order. He dealt with some of the allies harshly, while others, including Athens, whose high culture he greatly admired, received lenient treatment. In addition, he demanded that all Greeks take part in a confederacy that he would lead. The general terms were fairly simple. Macedonia would provide security for and maintain peace in Greece, and in return the city-states would contribute soldiers and other personnel to Philip when he needed them.

Most Greeks detested this new arrangement. But for the moment all recognized the futility of resistance. And many Greeks soon found themselves caught up in preparations for an invasion of the Persian Empire, Philip's next big project. But Philip was not destined to guide this massive undertaking. In 336 B.C. he was stabbed to death by a disgruntled Macedonian nobleman. Alexander took his father's place as king of Macedonia and captain-general of the new Greek confederacy.

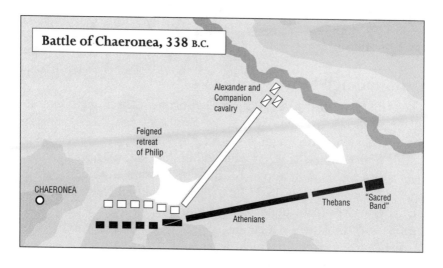

Battle of Chaeronea, 338 B.C.

Fascinated by Oratory

Many Greeks rejoiced upon hearing that Philip was dead, but few more than Demosthenes, who had for years openly opposed Philip and his policies. Although the two men were the same age, their backgrounds and experiences were very different. Whereas Philip was a royal prince who gained power by inheritance, Demosthenes had to work hard to make a name for himself in the competitive political arena of Athens's open democracy.

Demosthenes' father, a furniture maker who also crafted swords and kitchen knives, died when the boy was only seven. And the men named as guardians in the will mismanaged the estate and eventually left the young man nearly penniless. Demosthenes tried several times to sue them in court. He finally succeeded in getting a conviction, but got back only a tiny portion of his lost property.

Meanwhile, Demosthenes directed much of his time and energy to learning to be an orator. According to Plutarch, he was fascinated by the speakers he witnessed pleading cases in court and "he abandoned all other studies and all the normal pastimes of boyhood, and threw himself wholeheartedly into the practice of oratory."[42] Although the young man's voice was weak and his pronunciation marred by a lisp, he was determined to succeed. Describing his strenuous effort to improve, Plutarch wrote:

> He corrected his lisp and indistinct articulation by holding pebbles in his mouth while he recited long speeches and he strengthened his voice by running or walking uphill, speaking as he went, and by reciting speeches or verses in a single breath. Besides this, he kept a large mirror in his house and would stand in front of it while he went through his exercises.[43]

Denouncing Philip

These diligent efforts paid off, as Demosthenes became the greatest of all Greek orators. At first, he gained fame locally for writing speeches for the litigants at trials and sometimes prosecuting public figures himself. What vaulted him into international prominence was his strident and unbending opposition to the increasing aggressions of Philip II. In 352 B.C. Demosthenes delivered the first of his great speeches denouncing Philip, appropriately called the *Philippics*. "Observe, Athenians, the height to which the fellow's insolence has soared," Demosthenes said.

This drawing shows Demosthenes delivering one of his anti-Philip speeches (the Philippics) *to a group of Athenians.*

He leaves you no choice of action or inaction; he blusters and talks big . . . [and] he cannot rest content with what he has conquered; he is always taking in more, everywhere casting his net around us, while we sit idle and do nothing. When, Athenians, will you take the necessary action? What are you waiting for? Until you are compelled, I presume.[44]

Demosthenes naturally grew frustrated when these words seemed to fall on deaf ears. But he refused to give up, for he clearly saw the danger Philip posed to the freedom and independence of the traditional city-states. Philip soon moved on Olynthus, a prosperous northern Aegean city; and when the Olynthians appealed

Demosthenes rails against Philip in one of the Olynthiacs, *speeches denouncing Philip's aggression against the city of Olynthus.*

to Athens for aid, Demosthenes dutifully delivered three major speeches (the *Olynthiacs*) calling on Athens and other city-states to stop Philip. "What better time or occasion could you find than the present, men of Athens?" the orator asked.

> When will you do your duty, if not now? Has not your enemy already captured all our strongholds? . . . Is not Philip our enemy? And in possession of our property? And a barbarian? Is any description too bad for him?[45]

Dogged Attempts to Preserve Freedom

Demosthenes delivered his *Second Philippic* in 344 B.C. and his third in 341. Yet still his countrymen and most other Greeks were slow to act against the onrushing Macedonian menace. So Demosthenes took it upon himself to organize an anti-Philip coalition, with Athens and Thebes the major members. Decked out in armor and bearing a spear and sword, the orator stood in the Athenian ranks on the field of Chaeronea in 338. He also took part in the ignoble Athenian retreat.

After the battle, the Athenians chose Demosthenes to give the funeral oration over their dead. This was widely seen as a confirmation that the orator's countrymen did not blame him for the defeat, despite the fact that he had persuaded them to fight Philip. One of Demosthenes' friends went so far as to propose bestowing a golden crown on him for his years of service to the state. But his longtime political opponent, the orator Aeschines, objected, blaming Demosthenes for all of Athens's recent troubles. In 330 B.C. the matter came to a head with Demosthenes' delivery of the magnificent speech "On the Crown," which defended his anti-Macedonian crusade and denounced Aeschines for taking bribes from Philip.

In the years that followed, Demosthenes continued to oppose the Macedonian dominance of Greece. After Alexander died in 323 B.C. (in faraway Babylon), the orator got involved in a plot to topple Antipater, the Macedonian general then in charge of Greece. The plan failed and Demosthenes fled Athens. In 322 B.C. he took his own life by drinking poison rather than be captured. The Athenians, who never forgot him, his vast talents, and his dogged efforts to preserve their freedom, later raised a bronze statue to him. On its base appeared the words: "If only your strength had been equal, Demosthenes, to your wisdom, never would Greece have been ruled by a Macedonian."[46]

CHAPTER 7

Alexander and Ptolemy Lead the Greeks into the East

Philip II died before his two greatest dreams were fulfilled. These visions—the subordination of the city-state to large-scale monarchy and the spread of Greek power and culture into the Near East—did come to pass. But the task of implementing them fell to Philip's son, Alexander, and to Alexander's own immediate successors. In the space of only two generations, armies of Greek soldiers, administrators, and artisans transformed huge portions of the known world into sprawling Greek-ruled enclaves. In these kingdoms, including Ptolemaic Egypt, founded and ruled by Alexander's general Ptolemy (TAW-luh-mee), the non-Greek populations continued to live and work as they had for centuries. The difference was that now they had to follow the laws and fight in the armies of Greek, rather than native, monarchs. The term Hellenistic, used to describe these kingdoms and the age of their dominance, means "Greek-like" and refers to this overlaying of Eastern cultures with a thin veneer of Greek culture. The Hellenistic world created by Ptolemy and Alexander's other successors appeared, at least for a while, to be a brave new world in which Greek horizons would be limitless.

An Early Sense of Self-Importance

The concept of limitless horizons was certainly a part of Alexander's worldview from an early age. He was born in 356 B.C., the son of Olympias, a princess of the small northern Greek kingdom of Epirus and one of Philip's seven wives. The boy excelled at his studies and early on displayed a strong sense of self-importance, as well as a driving ambition to achieve great deeds. It is unclear how much of this attitude was inspired by Philip, how much by Olympias, and how much by Alexander's teachers.

One of these teachers was Aristotle, who tutored the boy in science, ethics, and literature. Aristotle also gave him a copy of Homer's *Iliad*, which Alexander kept with him for the rest of his life. The young man's belief that certain special humans are fated by the gods to achieve great deeds and everlasting fame may have derived from, or was at least bolstered by, his deep admiration for Achilles, the *Iliad's* central figure. Achilles consciously chose a brief life of fame and glory over a long one of obscurity. And the second-century A.D. Greek historian Arrian, whose history is the principal surviving source about Alexander, claimed that Alexander made a similar choice. "Those who endure hardship and danger are the ones who achieve glory," Alexander said (according to Arrian), "and the most gratifying thing is to live with courage and to die leaving behind eternal renown."[47]

Considering his premature preoccupation with achieving notoriety, it is not surprising that Alexander wanted to go along on Philip's frequent military campaigns. But Philip insisted that the boy was too young. In his own biography of Alexander, Plutarch captured the boy's frustration this way:

Whenever he heard that Philip had captured some famous city or won an overwhelming victory, Alexander would show no pleasure at the news, but would declare to his friends, "Boys, my father will forestall me in everything.

Achilles slays the Trojan Hector in an episode from Homer's Iliad. *Alexander saw himself as the new Achilles.*

There will be nothing great or spectacular for you and me to show the world."[48]

Alexander Becomes King

It was not until Alexander was sixteen that his father finally gave him a chance to prove himself. Just before leaving for a campaign, Philip gave the young man the title of regent, which endowed him with the authority to run the country while Philip was away. Alexander swiftly showed his leadership abilities. Both his father and other leading Macedonians were impressed when he crushed a local rebellion and established a new city. No doubt this convinced Philip that his son was ready to stand beside him in battle, and in 338 B.C. the eighteen-year-old Alexander commanded the Macedonian cavalry in Philip's great victory over the city-states at Chaeronea.

A much bigger test for Alexander came two years later when an assassin struck Philip down. Suddenly, the young man was king of Macedonia and captain-general of the new Greek confederacy Philip had recently forged. Some Greeks made the mistake of underestimating Alexander because of his youth and rebelled against Macedonian authority. But he wasted no time in showing that he was both an able administrator and a ruthless opponent. Alexander punished Thebes, the main hotbed of the insurrection, unmercifully, demolishing most of the city, killing most of the men, and selling the women and children into slavery.

Soon after ordering this atrocity, one of many he would commit in his career, Alexander turned his attention to the invasion of Persia, which Philip had been planning for some time. In 334 B.C. the young king marched into Asia Minor at the head of a mixed army of Macedonians and other Greeks numbering about thirty-two thousand infantry and five thousand cavalry.[49] Alexander proceeded to use what were essentially Philip's army and tactics in effective, occasionally brilliant ways, sometimes creating new tactics as he went along. His first major victory occurred at the Granicus River, in northwestern Asia Minor. There he defeated an army led by some of the local Persian governors, who had gathered their forces to block his path.

The young conqueror next moved southward. In the following year, at Issus, in Syria, he encountered a larger army commanded by the Persian king himself, Darius III. Alexander was once again victorious, although Darius managed to escape. Heading farther south, the Greeks captured the island city of Tyre, on the Pales-

This painting by Peter Connolly depicts Alexander leading his men across the Granicus River toward the Persian lines.

tinian coast, and then liberated Egypt, which the Persians had ruled for about two centuries. There, in the Nile Delta, Alexander initiated construction of a new city. Called Alexandria after its founder, it was destined to become one of the greatest commercial and cultural centers of the ancient world.

To India and Back

Rich in human and natural resources, Egypt was an important prize for Alexander. But he coveted much more. Early in 331 B.C. he led his army northeastward into the Persian heartland (in what are now Iraq and Iran), where Darius waited with another army. At Gaugamela, about 270 miles north of Babylon, a tremendous battle took place. "With shouts of encouragement to one another," Plutarch wrote, the Macedonian cavalry "charged the enemy at full speed and the phalanx rolled forward like a flood." During the assault, Alexander saw Darius and charged right at him. Terrified, the Persian monarch "abandoned his chariot and his armor, mounted a mare . . . and rode away"[50] After winning the battle, Alexander chased his adversary for miles. But once again Darius escaped. Later, however, some of the Persian king's own followers betrayed him and tried to trade him to Alexander in exchange for leniency for themselves. In the end, they slew Darius, and Alexander, outraged by their disloyalty and audacity, slew them.

In the next few years Alexander finished his conquest of the Persian realm. The relentless march took him and his troops into the vast desert regions now occupied by eastern Iran and Afghanistan and finally, late in 327 B.C., to the borders of India. There, one of the local kings—Porus—resisted the intruders but met defeat at the Hydaspes River (May 326 B.C.). Alexander wanted to continue his conquests in Asia. However, his men, exhausted and homesick, refused to go any farther. Reluctantly, therefore, Alexander ordered the army's return to Babylon, a difficult journey during which many soldiers died.

The expedition's survivors reached Babylon in the spring of 323 B.C. and shortly afterward, on June 10, Alexander died unexpectedly (perhaps of malaria) at the age of only thirty-three. Arrian later said of him:

> He had a great personal beauty, invincible power of endurance, and a keen intellect. He was brave and adventurous. . . . He had an uncanny instinct for the right course in a difficult and complex situation. . . . In arming and equipping troops and in his military dispositions he was always masterly.[51]

In the interest of proper balance, it should be added that Alexander was also very self-centered, stubborn, and often unnecessarily brutal and inhumane.

Companion and Adviser to the King

The empire Alexander had created in only a few years was the largest the world had yet seen. But he failed to name an heir before he died. So a great power struggle erupted among his leading generals and governors, including Perdiccas, Seleucus, Antigonus, Cassander, Lysimachus, and Ptolemy, to name only a few. These men, who became known as the "Successors," waged a series of battles and wars that lasted almost forty years.

The successor whose legacy and influence lasted the longest and affected the most people was Ptolemy. His father, Lagus, had been a Macedonian aristocrat at Philip's court, and his mother, Arsinoë

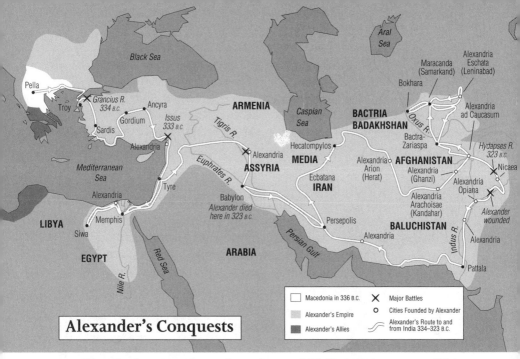

(ar-SIN-oh-eh), may have been one of Philip's mistresses. (This caused rumors, largely unsubstantiated, that Ptolemy was Philip's illegitimate son.) Not much else is known about Ptolemy's early life except that he was about ten years older than Alexander and one of his closest boyhood friends.

This closeness later caused Ptolemy some considerable discomfort and embarrassment. Shortly before Philip's assassination in 336 B.C., Philip and Alexander had a falling out, ostensibly over Alexander's choosing a bride that his father did not approve of. It is also possible that this was an official lie designed to cover up a failed plot by Alexander to oust Philip and take the throne. Either way, the angry king punished Alexander by banishing several of his companions, including Ptolemy. After Philip's death, though, Alexander recalled and reinstated Ptolemy and the others.

Soon after this episode, Ptolemy followed Alexander on his momentous campaigns in Persia. Ptolemy not only served on the king's general staff of close advisers but also kept a journal that was later published as an account of the expedition. This book, which regrettably is now lost, became one of the major sources used later by Arrian and other chroniclers of Alexander's life and deeds.

Ptolemy Establishes a Power Base

Ptolemy's personal profile and power expanded considerably following Alexander's death in 323 B.C. At a meeting of the dead king's closest advisers and generals, before they began quarreling,

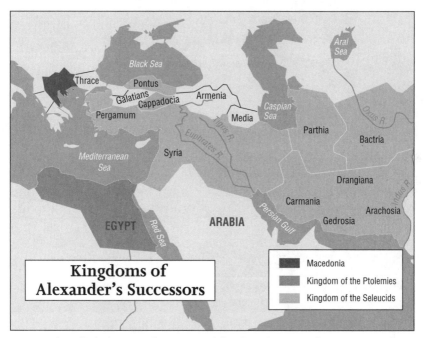

Kingdoms of Alexander's Successors

- Macedonia
- Kingdom of the Ptolemies
- Kingdom of the Seleucids

it was decided that Ptolemy would take charge of Egypt. Gathering a contingent of troops loyal to him, he immediately hurried to that land and confronted Cleomenes, a Macedonian whom Alexander had left in charge of collecting taxes several years before. Ptolemy found that in Alexander's absence the greedy and corrupt Cleomenes had overtaxed the populace and extorted money from local priests and nobles. Wasting no time, Ptolemy executed Cleomenes and assumed complete control of the country.

Like several of the other successors based in other sectors of Alexander's empire, Ptolemy wanted to establish a permanent basis of power and prestige for himself. With this in mind, he boldly sent soldiers to seize Alexander's body, which was on its way back to Greece from Babylon. Ptolemy ordered that the corpse be placed in a golden coffin, which lay first in the city of Memphis before finding a more permanent home in Alexandria. To many Greeks, control of Alexander's remains gave Ptolemy a strong appearance of legitimacy and credibility as the dead conqueror's most important successor.

Ptolemy did not immediately declare himself king of Egypt, however. At first, he ruled the country in Alexander's name while struggling with the other successors for control of vast sectors of the Near East. The first successor who tried to dislodge Ptolemy from power was Perdiccas, who was defeated and repulsed in the Nile Delta in 321 B.C. Antigonus proved much more formidable; in

72

315, Ptolemy joined a shaky coalition of successors against Antigonus and his son, Demetrius. The latter defeated Ptolemy's fleet in 306. But Ptolemy achieved revenge by playing a major role in a gigantic battle fought in 301 at Ipsus, in Asia Minor. Antigonus and Demetrius were disastrously defeated, leaving Ptolemy entrenched more strongly than ever in Egypt.

"Savior" of the World

Indeed, in these years Ptolemy became increasingly confident that he could not be dislodged from the kingdom he had carved out. It included not only Egypt but parts of Palestine and Asia Minor and the large island of Cyprus. Three years before his victory at Ipsus, Ptolemy declared himself king of Egypt. And he celebrated the win at Ipsus by adding the title of Soter, or "Savior," to his name. In the process, he founded a new Egyptian ruling family, the first Greek one the country had ever had—the Ptolemaic dynasty.

This coin, minted about 300 B.C., following the battle of Ipsus, bears the image of Ptolemy I, founder of the Ptolemaic dynasty.

From his capital at Alexandria, Ptolemy ruled Egypt as it had always been ruled, as an absolute monarchy. With the exception of the royal family now being Greek, for the average Egyptian nothing had changed significantly. Native farmers continued to labor in the fields and many of them to work part-time on government building projects. Meanwhile, increasing numbers of Greeks migrated to Alexandria. Encouraged by Ptolemy, Greek merchants, soldiers, and administrators created a privileged class that exploited the natives, most of whom were looked on by the Greeks as inferior.

In the years following Ipsus, Ptolemy also made Alexandria the urban showcase of the known world. He began work on an enormous and splendid palace complex; established the Museum, a university where scholars from many lands converged; and erected the Great Library, which eventually housed the works of all the known authors. Bringing Greek culture to the Near East had been one of Alexander's major goals. And Ptolemy did his part to fulfill it. When he died in 283 B.C. at the age of about eighty-four, Ptolemy lorded over one of the most powerful empires on earth, one that was destined to shape the history of both Europe and the Near East for nearly three centuries to come.

CHAPTER 8

Cleopatra and Other Queens Seek Power in a Man's World

During the Hellenistic Age that followed Alexander's conquests and death, the Greek world experienced a series of profound cultural changes. The city-states declined in importance and influence, for example, overshadowed by the large Greek monarchies that sprang up in the eastern Mediterranean and Near East. At the same time, artistic expression—painting, sculpture, and so forth—became more realistic (as opposed to the more idealized styles of the Classical Age).

There was also an increased appreciation for and emphasis placed on the rights, needs, and feelings of individual Greeks. This included women, who in some areas experienced a measured sort of liberation. Many women who could not do so before could now own, inherit, and bequeath property; give and receive loans; make their own marriage contracts; divorce their husbands at will; and become business owners.

It was still largely a man's world, however, for no Greek land—whether city-state or monarchy—granted its female citizenry the political rights to vote or hold public office. As had been true throughout Greece's long history, men held the positions of real power. Yet there are exceptions to every rule. For a handful of Greek women these exceptions came in Hellenistic times with the rise of some colorful and capable queens in the royal houses of the great monarchies. These privileged women often exercised considerable influence over their kingly husbands and sons, and occasionally a Hellenistic queen wielded real power. Unarguably the most prominent and famous example was Cleopatra VII, the last ruler of Egypt's Ptolemaic dynasty. For a few brief historical moments, she came close to holding political and military authority over much of the known world.

The Macedonian Queens

All cultural movements are based on earlier precedents. In the case of the influential Hellenistic queens, the models they followed were a series of strong-willed, often manipulative women in the royal family of the Macedonian kingdom that had produced Philip and Alexander. In ancient Macedonia, Michael Grant points out,

> queens of terrifying force had . . . made their appearance in earlier times. In the Macedonian royal family, the relation between mother and son was much stronger than the relation between husband and wife, so that a Macedonian queen stopped at nothing to secure the succession of her own son, which would bring her a dominant position in the state.[52]

Of these grasping Macedonian queens, Alexander's grandmother, Eurydice, and his mother, Olympias, were prime examples. Like him, both were ambitious, ruthless, and shrewd; and both owned their own lands and administered considerable wealth

This drawing is based on a stone bas-relief showing Olympias with her illustrious son, Alexander.

without the guidance of men. Eurydice, who hailed from the ancient Balkan kingdom of Illyria, married Macedonia's King Amyntas III and gave him three sons—Alexander II, Perdiccas, and Philip II. After Amyntas died in 370 B.C., she entered into a series of court intrigues that ensured that each of her sons would achieve the throne; at the same time, political enemies who got in the way ended up dead or banished.

Olympias exercised even more influence than her mother-in-law. Born a princess of Epirus, she married Philip in 357 B.C., two years after he secured the throne; and the following year she gave birth to Alexander, the future conqueror of Persia. Two years later she had a daughter named Cleopatra (a common Macedonian name). While Philip was away on his frequent campaigns, Olympias saw to the education of her children and forged strong personal bonds with them. Moreover, evidence suggests that she came to despise Philip and steadily turned Alexander against his father. This may explain some ancient rumors that said she engineered the plot (perhaps with Alexander's assistance) to assassinate Philip in 336.

Whether or not these rumors were true, Olympias took full advantage of Alexander's departure for Persia to further her own aims and ambitions. She got into a power struggle with Antipater, the man Alexander had left in charge of Macedonia. When it became clear that she could not eliminate Antipater, she withdrew to Epirus and ruled that kingdom despotically for more than a decade. Later, after Alexander's untimely death, Olympias jockeyed for ultimate power in Macedonia until one of Alexander's successors, Cassander, out of genuine fear of her tenacity and influence, had her killed.

The Shrewd and Resourceful Arsinoë

Several Hellenistic queens followed the example set by Eurydice, Olympias, and other Macedonian queens, namely that of a strong female authority figure fighting for power and recognition in a man's world. Of the great Greek monarchies that dominated the age, Ptolemaic Egypt produced the largest number of these ambitious, talented women. One of the most remarkable was Arsinoë II, wife and sister of the second Ptolemaic king, Ptolemy II Philadelphus (reigned 283–246 B.C.). Intelligent, resourceful, shrewd, and calculating, Arsinoë often overshadowed her husband, and her contributions to the kingdom's strength and prosperity were almost as great as those of her illustrious father, Ptolemy I Soter.

The so-called Gonzaga cameo shows King Ptolemy II Philadelphus and his sister and second wife Arsinoë II.

It was Arsinoë's father who arranged for her, in about 300 B.C., when she was sixteen, to marry another of Alexander's successors, Lysimachus. Lysimachus had consolidated a large kingdom in Thrace, and the marriage was designed to improve relations between the two kings. Though her new husband was more than forty years her senior, she gave him three sons. She also convinced him to kill his son by a previous marriage so that one of her own children would be next in line for the throne. These plans did not come to fruition, however. In 281 B.C. Lysimachus's enemies killed him and Arsinoë escaped with her sons (by dressing them and herself as beggars and mingling with the commoners on the waterfront).

At the age of about forty, Arsinoë returned to Egypt. There, she persuaded her brother, Ptolemy II (who was now king), to exile his first wife, after which Ptolemy and Arsinoë were married (following an Egyptian custom of royal unions between siblings). In the years that followed, she exerted a major influence on her husband, who was otherwise a weak ruler. Thanks in large part to Arsinoë's advice and inspiration, the kingdom expanded its territory in the eastern Mediterranean and became richer and more prestigious than ever. Arsinoë's personal prestige and power is evidenced by the facts that her portrait appeared on coins alongside her husband's and that she was deified (proclaimed a god) as an incarnation of the Egyptian goddess Isis. When she died suddenly at the age of forty-five, the grieving Ptolemy issued commemorative coins in her honor.

A Young Queen in a Troubled Realm

Other female members of the Ptolemaic family distinguished themselves in one way or another in the years that followed. After the death of her husband in 180 B.C., Cleopatra I ruled Egypt essentially alone, as regent for her son, Ptolemy VI. And later in the same century, another Ptolemy, Cleopatra Thea, married three different kings of the Seleucid kingdom (encompassing Syria and Mesopotamia) and mothered two more. Long influential behind the scenes in the Seleucid court, she was the only Seleucid queen whose image appeared alone on coins.

Surviving busts of Cleopatra VII are likely later idealized portraits. It remains uncertain what she really looked like.

Despite the fame and influence achieved by these and other Hellenistic queens, it was the last of the many Greek queens bearing the name of Cleopatra who became the most renowned woman of ancient times. Cleopatra VII was born in Egypt in 69 B.C. By this time, the Ptolemaic realm had drastically declined in

79

power. The last surviving large Greek monarchy (the others having been absorbed by Rome), the kingdom and its rulers were now no more than pawns in the ongoing power struggles among the strongest Romans of the day. Indeed, Cleopatra's father, the weak Ptolemy XII, was able to maintain his feeble hold on power in Egypt only through bribing such men.

Cleopatra turned out to be a good deal more cunning, resourceful, and successful than her father, however. Politically astute from a young age, she demonstrated that the key to obtaining and holding on to power was to form real and meaningful alliances with Roman leaders. Her first such partnership was with the famous politician and military general Julius Caesar. The circumstances leading to their meeting were that Ptolemy XII died in 51 B.C., leaving Cleopatra, then eighteen, and her ten-year-old brother, Ptolemy XIII, as joint rulers of Egypt. Almost immediately a power struggle erupted, as Ptolemy's chief adviser, Pothinus, disliked the young queen and wished to see the boy become sole ruler. In September 49 B.C. they drove her from Alexandria and into hiding. But the following year Caesar, who had just defeated his chief rival in a huge Roman civil war, arrived in Egypt. In a bold move, Cleopatra smuggled herself into the palace to meet him. According to Plutarch's account:

> Since there seemed to be no other way of getting in, she stretched herself out at full length inside a sleeping bag, and Apollodorus [her servant], after tying up the bag, carried it indoors to Caesar. This little trick of Cleopatra's, which showed her provocative impudence, is said to have been the first thing about her which captivated Caesar.[53]

An Efficient and Just Ruler

Caesar and Cleopatra became lovers, and he and his troops backed her in her struggle against her brother. Clearly no match for Caesar, Ptolemy and Pothinus were soon dead and the young queen was back on the throne. Caesar remained in Egypt for several more months, during which time he and Cleopatra further cemented their relationship and alliance. When he left Alexandria to put down a rebellion in Asia Minor in 47 B.C., she was carrying his child.

About a year later, after defeating the last of his rivals, Caesar invited Cleopatra and the new baby, a boy, to Rome. The second-century Roman historian Suetonius wrote that Caesar gave her "high titles and rich presents [and] even allowed her to call the son

A modern painting depicts the famous moment when Cleopatra, who had sneaked into the palace, revealed herself to Julius Caesar.

whom she had borne him by his own name." [54] Thus, the boy became popularly known as Caesarion, although his Egyptian title was Ptolemy XV.

Caesar never got the chance to get to know Caesarion very well, because in March 44 B.C. he was assassinated by a group of disgruntled Roman senators. The grieving Cleopatra immediately took her son back to Egypt. There she went about the business of administering the country, a task that evidence suggests she performed with distinction. She managed the economy well, expanded Egypt's already large agricultural output (which eliminated food shortages and lowered food prices), and treated her people with justice. A surviving decree from her reign reads in part:

> Nobody should demand of them [the farmers] anything above the essential Royal Dues [basic taxes]. . . . Nor shall

Roman soldiers discover Cleopatra's suicide, which robbed Octavian of the chance to march her in chains through Rome.

any new tax be required of them. But when they have once paid the essential Dues, in kind [in the form of goods and services] or in cash, for cornland and for vineland . . . they shall not be molested for anything further, on any pretext whatever. Let it be done accordingly, and this [decree] put up in public, according to Law.[55]

What Might Have Been

Though an efficient and thoughtful ruler, Cleopatra was also an ambitious one and soon found herself drawn back into Roman power politics. In late summer 41 B.C., Mark Antony (Marcus Antonius), Caesar's former lieutenant, summoned her to a meeting in Asia Minor. To further his own military career and prestige, Antony needed ships and grain, which Egypt possessed in abundance. Soon, however, he found himself as captivated by Cleopatra as Caesar had been. The two became lovers and formed an alliance.

It was not long before Cleopatra's and Antony's military, logistical, and personal resources were put to a severe test. A new Roman civil war erupted, this time between Antony and Caesar's adopted son, Octavian. It essentially came down to a struggle for control of much of the known world, for Antony and Cleopatra held sway over the eastern portions of Rome's vast empire, Octavian commanded the western portions, and the winner would take all. Perhaps to the surprise of most of those involved, the outcome of this great struggle was decided by a single battle. At Actium, in western Greece, in September 31 B.C., Octavian's fleet decisively defeated that of the lovers, who escaped and fled back to Egypt.

Octavian eventually followed. As his forces bore down on Alexandria, Antony's last few loyal troops deserted him, leaving him and Cleopatra virtually defenseless. Fear gripped the city, which fell into chaos, and in the confusion someone mistakenly told Antony that Cleopatra was dead. He reacted by falling on his sword, although he did not die right away. Servants soon reunited him with Cleopatra and he died in her arms. Afterward, Octavian captured her. But before he could enact his revenge on her, she took her own life (perhaps through the bite of a poisonous snake).

In her twenty-one years as Egypt's queen, Cleopatra had shown that a woman ruler could be as politically skilled, audacious, and courageous as any male ruler. After her passing, Octavian and others tried to discredit and marginalize her. But they could not erase the memory of her extraordinary personality and deeds or destroy the future vision she stood for and dreamed of—a world in which men and women might meet on an even playing field. In the words of noted historian Peter Green, in a sense "Cleopatra achieved her dying wish." Only her famous predecessor Alexander the Great, Green writes,

> eclipsed the mesmeric [hypnotic] fascination that she exercised down the centuries, and still exercises, upon the [Western] imagination, the perennial symbol of what, had Actium gone the other way, might have been a profoundly different world.[56]

CHAPTER 9

Polybius and Plutarch Record Greek Deeds for Posterity

Octavian's defeat of Cleopatra and absorption of Egypt into the Roman realm in the late first century B.C. was the final step in Rome's conquest of the Greek lands, which had begun nearly two centuries before. In 200 B.C. the Romans launched their first major assault on the Macedonian kingdom (the larger Hellenistic version of which had been founded less than a century before by the grandson of Alexander's successor Antigonus). And thereafter, the major Hellenistic Greek states fell to Rome like proverbial dominoes, eventually leaving the Romans in complete control of the Mediterranean world.

The Greek historian Polybius witnessed and recorded for posterity some of the opening salvos of this eclipse of the Greeks by Rome. He provided a unique perspective because he became close to some of the major Roman figures of his day; in the process he came to respect his adversaries and was to some degree "Romanized." In his writings can be seen the first Greek admission that the Romans had special qualities and perhaps a divine destiny to rule the world. In the opening of his masterwork, the *Histories*, Polybius writes:

> There can surely be nobody so petty or so apathetic in his outlook that he has no desire to discover by what means and under what system of government the Romans succeeded in only [a few] years in bringing under rule almost the whole of the inhabited world, an achievement which is without parallel in human history.[57]

Another important Greek writer who came to respect the Romans and passed on to future generations a chronicle of their mastery over Greece was Plutarch of Chaeronea. Born shortly after the conquest of the Greek sphere had been completed, he even became a Roman citizen. Plutarch was a prodigious writer, and many of his works have survived. The best known is the *Parallel Lives*, a compilation of biographies of Greek and Roman figures that contains invaluable information about Greco-Roman history that otherwise would have been lost. (Much of the treatise was based on ancient works that did not survive antiquity.)

In a way, then, Polybius and Plutarch are like bookends on either end of the final period of Greek autonomy in the ancient world. One witnessed the beginnings of the Greeks' fall; the other looked back on it as something regrettable but perhaps inevitable. Their importance lies in the fact that much of what is known about these momentous events was filtered through their pens.

The Achaean League and Polybius's Youth

Exactly when Polybius took up his pen is uncertain, as are the dates of his birth and death. The best guess is that he was born in the last years of the third century B.C., probably in 200, the year Rome invaded Greece for the first time. Polybius's birthplace was Megalopolis, located in the center of the Peloponnesus. At the time, the city was part of the Achaean League. This alliance of ten Peloponnesian cities had been established in 280 B.C. for the purpose of mutual protection against the ambitious Macedonian kingdom, which controlled most of mainland Greece north of the Peloponnesus.

This engraving purportedly shows Plutarch, but his true appearance is unknown.

That Polybius would play a prominent role in Achaean politics seemed assured from the start. His father, Lycortas, a wealthy landowner, was a popular politician with close ties to Philopoemen, leader of the league. And in 182 B.C., the young Polybius was honored to be chosen to carry Philopoemen's ashes in the great man's

Some scholars think this sculpture depicts the Greek historian Polybius.

funeral procession. Later, Polybius wrote a biography of Philopoemen. The work has not survived but was likely the main source for Plutarch's biography of the same person, which *has* survived.

Not much is known about the next decade or so of Polybius's life. Among the few recorded facts is that in 181 B.C., when he was about nineteen or twenty, the Achaean League chose him to serve in a delegation to Egypt, then ruled by King Ptolemy V. But the trip was canceled when news came that Ptolemy had died suddenly. A few years later, Polybius was elected to the prestigious position of cavalry commander, only one step lower than general, the highest office in the league.

Polybius never attained the generalship, however, because the sudden intervention of the Romans into Achaean affairs abruptly changed his life. The Achaean League had for some time taken Rome's side against Macedonia, which the league had long distrusted and opposed. But as they watched the Romans crush and dismantle the Macedonian kingdom, the Achaeans grew increasingly worried about and antagonistic toward Rome's intrusion into Greek affairs. The Romans sensed that trouble was brewing. So, following their final defeat of Macedonia in 168 B.C., they took the precaution of deporting about a thousand prominent Achaeans as hostages to Italy. Polybius was among them.

An Honest, Accurate Historian

Polybius was detained by the Romans for sixteen years. However, he was fortunate in that he met the Roman aristocrat and future general Scipio Aemilianus, who took a liking to the young Greek.

In a funeral procession, the young Polybius carries the ashes of Philopoemen, a prominent statesman of the Achaean League.

This illustration depicts the Roman destruction of Carthage (at the climax of the Third Punic War), which Polybius witnessed firsthand.

"I only wish I may see the day when you will give me the first claim to your attention and join your life to mine," Scipio told Polybius, according to the latter. "From the moment of that conversation, the young man [Scipio] became inseparable from Polybius and preferred his company to any other."[58] Beginning in 151 B.C., Polybius accompanied Scipio on the young Roman's military campaigns in Spain and North Africa. And the two men stood together and watched Roman troops destroy Carthage (in what is now Tunisia) in 146, at the climax of the Third Punic War.

Eventually, Polybius was allowed to return to Greece. For a while, in the 140s B.C., he acted as an intermediary between the Achaeans and Romans, who had come to blows. This altercation ended with a Roman general dissolving the Achaean League.

Polybius then set about writing his forty-volume history of Rome (covering the period 220–146 B.C.). Of this major work, the first five volumes, plus fragments of several others, have survived. They show that his writing style is not as lively and appealing as that of Herodotus or Thucydides. But Polybius was an honest, thorough, and accurate historian. He died from a fall from a horse circa 118 B.C.

Polybius provided considerable analysis of and advice about historical methods, including his own. This exerted a strong influence on later Western historians. For example, he agreed with Thucydides that, except for witnessing an event himself, the soundest practice for a historian was to interview eyewitnesses. "Making first-hand inquiries . . . is the historian's most important duty," he stated.

> For since many events occur simultaneously in different places and it is impossible for the same man to be everywhere at once, and likewise impossible for him to have seen with his own eyes all the places in the world . . . the only course which remains . . . is to question as many people as possible, to believe such witnesses as are trustworthy, and to prove himself a good judge of the reports that reach him.[59]

Michael Grant sums up Polybius's other important contributions to the genre of historical writing this way:

> Without the writings of Polybius we would know very little indeed about the third and second centuries B.C. And what he has given us is a remarkable record of the growth of Roman power. Furthermore, one of his doctrines—that the "mixed" constitution which, in his view, was responsible for Rome's

success—exercised powerful political influence in the early days of the United States of America. John Adams frequently spoke of him, and it is principally because of Polybius that the Constitution of the United States contains the separate powers, limited by a system of balance and checks, which have contributed so largely to its continuing strength.[60]

Plutarch's Greco-Roman Symbiosis

Indeed, one of the hallmarks of Polybius's writings is his unabashed respect for Roman government and military methods, which he saw as the key factors in Rome's rise to dominion in the Mediterranean world. Plutarch was even more enamored of the Romans, though he was still extremely proud of his Greek roots. As one modern scholar puts it:

> He was a Greek who, while lacking national bias, was conscious of his Greekness, and by no means ashamed of it, and yet completely accepted the role of the Romans as the dominant power. He [openly] advocated the coming together of the two cultures.[61]

This is hardly surprising, for when Plutarch was born sometime between A.D. 45 and 50, his native region of Boeotia had been part of the Roman commonwealth for two centuries. Unlike Polybius, therefore, he did not know what it was like to grow up in an independent Greece, and his boyhood heroes were both Greeks and Romans. Plutarch's life continued to reflect a Greco-Roman symbiosis (merger or fusion). On the one hand, he was active in local politics in his native town of Chaeronea, and later in life he was involved in the priesthood at the shrine at Delphi, about fifteen miles west of his home.

At the same time, however, Plutarch became a Roman citizen, adopting the family name of a Roman friend, Lucius Mestrius Florus. Plutarch traveled to Rome at least twice, where he met many high-placed Romans (perhaps including the emperor Hadrian) and lectured widely. While in Rome, he was appointed an official diplomat to his native region in Greece. After traveling to Egypt and a number of other lands, where he gave more lectures to his fans (for he was by now a famous author), he returned to Chaeronea. He died there in about A.D. 120.

"A Genius for Making Greatness Stand Out"

What made Plutarch most famous in his own time, as well as in later ages, was his voluminous work, the *Parallel Lives*, which has survived almost complete. It consists of about fifty biographies of prominent Greek and Roman figures, mostly from past eras but also including a few who flourished during his lifetime. The biographies are not straightforward historical tracts because Plutarch's intention was to stress the character traits and moral attributes that had made his subjects great and famous. Nevertheless, his sources included hundreds of important ancient historical works that are now lost. So his biographies remain a priceless collection of information about Greco-Roman history from about 600 B.C. to A.D. 70.

Indeed, thousands of anecdotes in the *Lives* capture the details of events and scenes that would otherwise be lost forever. Cleopatra's magnificent entrance into the harbor at Tarsus, where Antony had summoned her in 41 B.C., is one of the most memorable:

> She came sailing up the river Cydnus in a barge with a stern of gold, its purple sails billowing in the wind, while her rowers caressed the water with oars of silver which dipped in time to the music of the flute, accompanied by pipes and lutes. Cleopatra herself reclined beneath a canopy of gold cloth, dressed as Venus [goddess of love] . . . while on either side . . . stood boys costumed as Cupids, who cooled her with fans. Instead of a crew, her barge was lined with the most beautiful of her waiting-women attired as [minor goddesses] . . . and all the while an indescribably rich perfume . . . wafted from the vessel to the river-banks. Great multitudes [of local people] accompanied this royal progress, some of them following the queen on both sides of the river from its very mouth, while others hurried down from the city of Tarsus to gaze at the sight.[62]

This passage demonstrates Plutarch's engaging writing style, which made the stories of his Greco-Roman heroes come alive for his own and future generations. Not surprisingly, a number of later plays and movies were based wholly or partly on his timeless biographies. The sixteenth-century translation of the *Parallel Lives* by Sir Thomas North became the main source for William Shakespeare's plays *Coriolanus, Julius Caesar,* and *Antony and Cleopatra,* for example. Regarding Plutarch's style and influence, one of his leading modern translators, the late Ian Scott-Kilvert, wrote:

> Plutarch has an unerring sense of the drama of men in great situations. His eye ranges over a wider field of

Cleopatra meets Antony at Tarsus, one of thousands of historical incidents that Plutarch chronicled in the Parallel Lives.

human action than any of the [ancient] classical historians. He surveys men's conduct in war, in council, in love, in the use of money . . . in religion, in the family. . . . Believing implicitly in the stature of his heroes, he has a genius for making greatness stand out in small actions. . . . Plutarch has engraved [countless scenes from the lives of prominent ancient figures] on the memory of posterity for all time. It was certainly this power of his to epitomize the moral grandeur of the ancient world which appealed most strongly to Shakespeare.[63]

The jobs of the historian and biographer are key to learning about and understanding the past. Without dedicated chroniclers like Polybius and Plutarch, therefore, the memorable deeds of Pericles, Philip, Alexander, Cleopatra, and other Greek shapers of the Western world would be lost forever in the mists of time. Consequently, people today who care to know about their ancient roots owe Herodotus, Thucydides, Xenophon, Polybius, Plutarch, and others like them an incalculable debt.

NOTES

Introduction: Keeping Alive the Spirit of People Long Dead

1. Charles Freeman, *The Greek Achievement: The Foundation of the Western World.* New York: Viking, 1999, p. 434.

2. Robert B. Kebric, *Greek People.* Mountain View, CA: Mayfield, 2001, p.v.

Chapter 1: Homer and Hesiod Define the Ancient Gods and Heroes

3. Richmond Lattimore, introduction to Homer, *Iliad*, trans. Richmond Lattimore. Chicago: University of Chicago Press, 1961 pp. 13–14.

4. Sarah B. Pomeroy et al., *Ancient Greece: A Political, Social, and Cultural History.* New York: Oxford University Press, 1999, p. 53.

5. Lattimore, introduction to *Iliad*, p. 54.

6. John A. Scott, "Homer Synonymous with Poet for the Greeks," in C.G. Thomas, ed., *Homer's History: Mycenaean or Dark Age?* New York: Holt, Rinehart and Winston, 1970, p. 112.

7. Hesiod, *Works and Days*, in *Hesiod and Theognis*, trans. Dorothea Wender. New York: Penguin, 1973, p. 65.

8. Herodotus, *The Histories*, trans. Aubrey de Sélincourt. New York: Penguin, 1972, p. 151.

Chapter 2: Themistocles and Pericles Lead Athens to Greatness

9. A.J. Podlecki, *The Life of Themistocles.* Montreal: McGill-Queen's University Press, 1975, p. 44.

10. Quoted in Thucydides, *The Peloponnesian War*, trans. Rex Warner. New York: Penguin, 1972, p. 148.

11. Plutarch, *Life of Themistocles*, in *Parallel Lives*, excerpted in *The Rise and Fall of Athens: Nine Greek Lives by Plutarch*, trans. Ian Scott-Kilvert. New York: Penguin, 1960, p. 77.

12. Plutarch, *Themistocles*, p. 78.

13. Plutarch, *Themistocles*, p. 80.

14. Plutarch, *Themistocles*, p. 81.

15. Aeschylus, *The Persians*, in *Aeschylus: Prometheus Bound,*

The Suppliants, Seven Against Thebes, The Persians, trans. Philip Vellacott. Baltimore: Penguin, 1961, p. 134.

16. Thucydides, *Peloponnesian War*, p. 79.

17. Plutarch, *Life of Pericles*, in *Rise and Fall of Athens*, p. 167.

18. Michael Grant, *The Classical Greeks*. New York: Scribner's, 1989, pp. 63–64.

19. Quoted in Thucydides, *Peloponnesian War*, p. 115.

20. Plutarch, *Pericles*, p. 177.

Chapter 3: Sophocles and Euripides Create Drama for the Ages

21. Plutarch, *Life of Cimon*, in *Rise and Fall of Athens*, p. 150.

22. Freeman, *Greek Achievement*, p. 249.

23. Aristophanes, *Frogs*, in *The Complete Plays of Aristophanes*, Moses Hadas, ed. New York: Bantam, 1962, p. 371.

24. Jacqueline de Romilly, *A Short History of Greek Literature*, trans. Lillian Doherty. Chicago: University of Chicago Press, 1985, pp. 80, 83–84.

25. Euripides, *Electra*, in *Euripides: Medea and Other Plays*, trans. Philip Vellacott. New York: Penguin, 1963, pp. 117–18.

Chapter 4: Thucydides and Xenophon Chronicle Greece's Wars

26. Herodotus, *Histories*, p. 41.

27. Thucydides, *Peloponnesian War*, p. 48.

28. Plutarch, *Cimon*, p. 144.

29. Thucydides, *Peloponnesian War*, p. 364.

30. Thucydides, *Peloponnesian War*, pp. 152, 154.

31. Thucydides, *Peloponnesian War*, p. 328.

32. Xenophon, *Memorabilia*, in *Xenophon: Conversations with Socrates*, trans. Hugh Tredennick and Robin Waterfield. New York: Penguin, 1990, pp. 70, 85.

33. Xenophon, *Anabasis*, trans. W.H.D. Rouse. New York: New American Library, 1959, p. 66.

34. Grant, *The Classical Greeks*, p. 159.

Chapter 5: Plato and Aristotle Explore the Frontiers of Knowledge

35. Alfred North Whitehead, *Process and Reality: An Essay in Cosmology*, ed. D.R. Griffin and D.W. Sherburne. New York: Free Press, 1978, p. 39.

36. Plato, *Laches*, in *Plato*, trans. Benjamin Jowett. Chicago: Encyclopaedia Britannica, 1952, p. 30.

37. Grant, *The Classical Greeks*, p. 219.

38. Freeman, *Greek Achievement*, p. 283.

Chapter 6: Philip and Demosthenes Clash over Greece's Freedom

39. Diodorus Siculus, *Library of History*, various trans. 12 vols. Cambridge, MA: Harvard University Press, 1962–1967, vol. 8, p. 103.

40. J.F.C. Fuller, *The Generalship of Alexander the Great*. New Brunswick, NJ: Rutgers University Press, 1960, p. 24.

41. Plutarch, *Life of Demosthenes*, in *The Age of Alexander: Nine Greek Lives by Plutarch*, trans. Ian Scott-Kilvert. New York: Penguin, 1973, p. 203.

42. Plutarch, *Demosthenes*, p. 192.

43. Plutarch, *Demosthenes*, p. 197.

44. Demosthenes, *First Philippic*, in *Olynthiacs, Philippics, Minor Speeches*, trans. J.H. Vince. Cambridge, MA: Harvard University Press, 1962, pp. 73–75.

45. Demosthenes, *Third Olynthiac*, in *Olynthiacs, Philippics, Minor Speeches*, p. 51.

46. Quoted in Plutarch, *Demosthenes*, p. 216.

Chapter 7: Alexander and Ptolemy Lead the Greeks into the East

47. Quoted in Arrian, *Anabasis Alexandri* 5.26, passage trans. Don Nardo.

48. Plutarch, *Life of Alexander*, in *Age of Alexander*, p. 256.

49. Of the infantry, some 12,000 were Macedonians comprising the phalanx, another 14,000 were from various allied Greek states, and the other 6,000 were archers and javelin men from the northern Aegean and the island of Crete. The cavalry broke down into roughly 2,000 Macedonian Companions, 1,800 horsemen from Thessaly (in central Greece), and a mixture of smaller allied contingents. For more detail, see Nicholas Sekunda and John Warry, *Alexander the Great: His Armies and Campaigns, 334–323 B.C.* London: Osprey, 1998.

50. Plutarch, *Alexander*, pp. 290–91.

51. Arrian, *Anabasis Alexandri*, published as *The Campaigns of Alexander*, trans. Aubrey de Sélincourt. New York: Penguin, 1971, pp. 395–96.

Chapter 8: Cleopatra and Other Queens Seek Power in a Man's World

52. Michael Grant, *From Alexander to Cleopatra: The Hellenistic World*. New York: Charles Scribner's Sons, 1982, pp. 194–95.

53. Plutarch, *Life of Caesar* in *Fall of the Roman Republic: Six Lives by Plutarch*, trans. Rex Warner. New York: Penguin, 1972, p. 290.

54. Suetonius, *Julius Caesar* in *Lives of the Twelve Caesars*, published as *The Twelve Caesars*, trans. Robert Graves, rev. Michael Grant. New York: Penguin, 1979, p. 36.

55. Quoted in Jack Lindsay, *Cleopatra*. London: Constable, 1970, pp. 127–28.

56. Peter Green, *Alexander to Actium: The Historical Evolution of the Hellenistic Age*. Berkeley and Los Angeles: University of California Press, 1990, p. 682.

Chapter 9: Polybius and Plutarch Record Greek Deeds for Posterity

57. Polybius, *Histories*, published as *Polybius: The Rise of the Roman Empire*, trans. Ian Scott-Kilvert. New York: Penguin, 1979, p. 41.

58. Polybius, *Histories*, p. 529.

59. Polybius, *Histories*, p. 431.

60. Michael Grant, *Greek and Roman Historians: Information and Misinformation*. London: Routledge, 1995, p. 12.

61. Grant, *Greek and Roman Historians*, p. 19.

62. Plutarch, *Life of Antony*, in *Makers of Rome: Nine Lives by Plutarch*, trans. Ian Scott-Kilvert. New York: Penguin, 1965, p. 293.

63. Ian Scott-Kilvert, introduction to *Rise and Fall of Athens*, p. 11.

CHRONOLOGY

B.C.

ca. 3000–1100
Greece's Bronze Age, in which people use tools and weapons made of bronze. Later Greeks will come to call the latter centuries of this period the "Age of Heroes."

ca. 1250
Traditional date for the Trojan War, possibly a Mycenaean raiding expedition later memorialized in Homer's epic poem the *Iliad*.

ca. 1100–800
Greece's Dark Age, in which poverty and illiteracy are at first widespread and city-states begin to emerge.

ca. 800–500
The Greek Archaic Age, characterized by the return of prosperity and literacy, rapid population growth, and intensive colonization of the Mediterranean and Black seas.

ca. 775
The Greek poet Homer is born.

ca. 700
Possible era in which the minor epic poet Hesiod flourishes.

534
Athens establishes the City Dionysia festival, which features the world's first dramatic contests.

ca. 523
The influential Athenian politician-general Themistocles is born.

ca. 508
Athens establishes the world's first democracy.

ca. 500–323
Greece's Classical Age, in which Greek arts, architecture, literature, and democratic reforms reach their height.

493
Themistocles is chosen archon (public administrator) in Athens.

490
The Athenians, aided by other Greeks, defeat a force of invading Persians at Marathon, northeast of Athens.

480
Themistocles engineers a major naval victory over the Persians at Salamis, southwest of Athens.

ca. 465
The democratic champion Pericles is elected to the post of general in Athens.

ca. 460–455
The great Athenian historian Thucydides is born.

431
The disastrous Peloponnesian War, which will engulf and exhaust almost all the city-states, begins; the Athenian playwright Euripides produces *Medea*.

430
A deadly plague strikes Athens, killing a large number of residents, including Pericles; the Athenian playwright Sophocles produces his great tragedy *Oedipus the King*.

427
The influential Athenian scholar-philosopher Plato is born.

406
Sophocles and Euripides die.

404
Athens surrenders, ending the great war.

401
The Athenian soldier-historian Xenophon takes part in the immortal March of the Ten Thousand, in which a small Greek army fights its way across western Asia.

399
The Athenian philosopher Socrates, mentor of Plato and Xenophon, is executed by the Athenian government.

ca. 387
Plato establishes the Academy, a school of higher learning, in Athens.

384
The great scholar-philosopher Aristotle is born.

359
Philip II ascends the throne of the northern Greek kingdom of Macedonia.

357
Philip marries Olympias, a princess of the northern Greek kingdom of Epirus.

356

Philip's son, Alexander III (later called "the Great"), is born.

352

The great Athenian orator Demosthenes delivers his First Philippic, a speech in which he denounces the aggressions of Philip II.

338

Philip and Alexander defeat an allied Greek army at Chaeronea, in central Greece.

336

Philip banishes Alexander's friend Ptolemy (whom Alexander will later recall); Philip is assassinated and Alexander ascends Macedonia's throne.

334

Alexander begins his conquest of the Persian Empire.

323

After carving out the largest empire the world has yet seen, Alexander dies in the Persian capital of Babylon.

ca. 323–30

Greece's Hellenistic Age, in which Alexander's successors divide his empire into several new kingdoms that frequently war among themselves, and Rome steadily gains control of the Greek world.

322

Demosthenes and Aristotle, both in exile from Athens, die.

304

Ptolemy, who assumed control of Egypt following Alexander's death, declares himself king of that land.

283

Ptolemy dies and is succeeded by his son, Ptolemy II Philadelphus.

ca. 200

The influential Greek historian Polybius is born.

69

The Ptolemaic Greek princess Cleopatra VII is born.

44

The Roman notable Julius Caesar, with whom Cleopatra has formed an alliance and had a child, is assassinated in the Roman Senate.

41

Cleopatra allies herself with Caesar's former assistant, Mark Antony.

31

Caesar's adopted son, Octavian (the future emperor Augustus), defeats

Cleopatra and Antony at Actium, in western Greece. Soon afterward the lovers commit suicide, leaving Octavian the most powerful figure in the known world.

30 B.C.–A.D. 476
Greece's Roman period, in which Rome rules the Greek lands.

A.D.
ca. 45–50
The influential Greek biographer and moralist Plutarch is born at Chaeronea.

FOR FURTHER READING

Books

Peter Connolly, *The Greek Armies*. Morristown, NJ: Silver Burdette, 1979. A fine, detailed study of Greek armor, weapons, and battle tactics, filled with colorful, accurate illustrations. Highly recommended.

———, *The Legend of Odysseus*. New York: Oxford University Press, 1986. A first-rate retelling of Homer's epics, the *Iliad* and the *Odyssey*, for young readers, amplified by many beautiful color paintings by the author, one of the greatest living illustrators of ancient times.

Robert B. Kebric, *Greek People*. Mountain View, CA: Mayfield, 2001. A superb overview of major ancient Greek figures from all walks of life.

Don Nardo, ed., *Cleopatra*. San Diego: Greenhaven, 2001. Presents a series of readable essays by noted historians about the last autonomous Greek ruler in antiquity.

———, *Philosophy and Science in Ancient Greece*. San Diego: Lucent, 2005. Chronicles the achievements of important ancient Greek scientists and thinkers, including Thales, Democritus, Aristarchus, Strato, Archimedes, Pytheas, Theophrastus, Euclid, and numerous others.

———, *Women of Ancient Greece*. San Diego: Lucent, 2000. Discusses the lives of ancient Greek women, including a number of notable ones.

John Warry, *Warfare in the Classical World*. Norman: University of Oklahoma Press, 1995. Filled with accurate and useful paintings, drawings, maps, and diagrams, this book provides useful information about the military leaders of the Greeks, Romans, and the peoples they fought.

Web Sites

PBS, "The Greeks: Crucible of Civilization" (www.pbs.org/ empires/ thegreeks). Excellent online resource based on the acclaimed PBS show. Has numerous links to sites containing information about ancient Greek figures, history, and culture.

Tufts University Department of the Classics, "Perseus Project" (www. perseus.tufts.edu). The most comprehensive online source about ancient Greece, with hundreds of links to all aspects of Greek history, life, and culture, supported by numerous photos of artifacts.

University of St. Andrews, Scotland, "Aristotle" (www-gap.dcs.st-and.ac.uk/~history/Mathematicians/Aristotle.html). A useful brief overview of Aristotle's life and teachings, with links to related topics and information.

Wikipedia Online Encyclopedia (http://en.wikipedia.org/wiki/Pericles). This online resource, inaugurated in 2001, contains many useful short biographies of ancient Greek figures, each featuring several links to related sites. Replace "Pericles" in the above Web address with another name to find synopses of Plato, Themistocles, Homer, Sophocles, Xenophon, Hesiod, Plutarch, and many others.

WORKS CONSULTED

Major Works

J.R. Ellis, *Philip II and Macedonian Imperialism*. New York: Thames and Hudson, 1977. One of the best modern studies of the rise of Philip and Macedonia.

Charles Freeman, *The Greek Achievement: The Foundation of the Western World*. New York: Viking, 1999. A well-written overview of ancient Greek civilization, touching on important people and cultural endeavors as well as history.

Michael Grant, *The Classical Greeks*. New York: Scribner's, 1989. A series of brief but very informative biographies of major ancient Greek figures by a noted scholar.

———, *The Rise of the Greeks*. New York: Macmillan, 1987. A superb examination of the rise of city-states in Greece, with detailed studies of nearly fifty separate states and the people who built them.

Peter Green, *Alexander of Macedon, 356–323 B.C.: A Historical Biography*. Berkeley and Los Angeles: University of California Press, 1991. One of the two or three best available overviews of Alexander and his exploits, by one of the leading classical historians of the past century.

———, *Alexander to Actium: The Historical Evolution of the Hellenistic Age*. Berkeley and Los Angeles: University of California Press, 1990. This huge tome is the most comprehensive study of Greece's Hellenistic Age written to date.

———, *The Greco-Persian Wars*. Berkeley and Los Angeles: University of California Press, 1996. An excellent overview of the Greek repulse of Persia from 490 to 479 B.C. and Themistocles' role in it.

Victor D. Hanson, *The Wars of the Ancient Greeks and Their Invention of Western Military Culture*. London: Cassell, 1999. A fine general study of ancient Greek military methods, battles, wars, and major military figures.

Lucy Hughes-Hallett, *Cleopatra: Histories, Dreams, and Distortions*. New York: HarperCollins, 1991. One of the best modern biographies of the famous Greek queen of Egypt.

Donald Kagan, *The Peloponnesian War*. New York: Viking, 2003. A renowned scholar masterfully summarizes the long and devastating conflict that involved nearly all of the Greek city-states. Thucydides and Xenophon figure prominently in this treatment.

Thomas R. Martin, *Ancient Greece: From Prehistoric to Hellenistic Times.* New Haven, CT: Yale University Press, 1996. One of the best general overviews of Greek history, culture, and leaders on the market.

Sarah B. Pomeroy et al., *Ancient Greece: A Political, Social, and Cultural History.* New York: Oxford University Press, 1999. A very well-organized, detailed, and insightful summary of ancient Greek civilization.

Graham Shipley, *The Greek World After Alexander, 323–30 B.C.* London: Routledge, 2000. A superior overview of the Hellenistic Age, successor states, and decline of Greece.

C.C.W. Taylor et al., *Greek Philosophers: Socrates, Plato, Aristotle.* New York: Oxford University Press, 2001. A fresh, insightful new look at the great triumvirate of ancient Greek philosophy.

C.G. Thomas, ed., *Homer's History: Mycenaean or Dark Age?* New York: Holt, Rinehart and Winston, 1970. An excellent compilation of scholarly essays about Homer and his great epic poems.

Other Important Works

Primary Sources

Aeschylus, *The Persians,* in *Aeschylus: Prometheus Bound, The Suppliants, Seven Against Thebes, The Persians.* Trans. Philip Vellacott. Baltimore: Penguin, 1961.

Aristophanes, *Frogs,* in *The Complete Plays of Aristophanes.* New York: Bantam, 1962.

Arrian, *Anabasis Alexandri,* published as *The Campaigns of Alexander.* Trans. Aubrey de Sélincourt. New York: Penguin, 1971.

Kenneth J. Atchity, ed., *The Classical Greek Reader.* New York: Oxford University Press, 1996.

Demosthenes, *Olynthiacs, Philippics, Minor Speeches.* Trans. J.H. Vince. Cambridge, MA: Harvard University Press, 1962.

Diodorus Siculus, *Library of History.* Various trans. 12 vols. Cambridge, MA: Harvard University Press, 1962–1967.

Euripides, assorted plays in *Euripides: Medea and Other Plays.* Trans. Philip Vellacott. New York: Penguin, 1963.

Herodotus, *The Histories.* Trans. Aubrey de Sélincourt. New York: Penguin, 1972.

Hesiod, *Works and Days*, in *Hesiod and Theognis*. Trans. Dorothea Wender. New York: Penguin, 1973.

Homer, *Iliad*. Trans. E.V. Rieu. Baltimore: Penguin, 1950; also trans. Richmond Lattimore. Chicago: University of Chicago Press, 1961.

———, *Odyssey*. Trans. E.V. Rieu. Baltimore: Penguin, 1961.

Plato, *Laches*, in *Plato*. Trans. Benjamin Jowett. Chicago: Encyclopaedia Britannica, 1952.

Plutarch, *Parallel Lives*, excerpted in *The Rise and Fall of Athens: Nine Greek Lives by Plutarch*. Trans. Ian Scott-Kilvert. New York: Penguin, 1960; also excerpted in *The Age of Alexander: Nine Greek Lives by Plutarch*. Trans. Ian Scott-Kilvert. New York: Penguin, 1973; *Fall of the Roman Republic: Six Lives by Plutarch*. Trans. Rex Warner. New York: Penguin, 1972; and *Makers of Rome: Nine Lives by Plutarch*. Trans. Ian Scott-Kilvert. New York: Penguin, 1965.

Polybius, *Histories*, published as *Polybius: The Rise of the Roman Empire*. Trans. Ian Scott-Kilvert. New York: Penguin, 1979.

Suetonius, *Lives of the Twelve Caesars*, published as *The Twelve Caesars*. Trans. Robert Graves. Rev. Michael Grant. New York: Penguin, 1979.

Thucydides, *The Peloponnesian War*. Trans. Rex Warner. New York: Penguin, 1972.

Xenophon, *Anabasis*. Trans. W.H.D. Rouse. New York: New American Library, 1959.

———, *Hellenica*, published as *A History of My Times*. Trans. Rex Warner. New York: Penguin, 1979.

———, *Memorabilia* and *Oeconomicus*, in *Xenophon: Conversations with Socrates*. Trans. Hugh Tredennick and Robin Waterfield. New York: Penguin, 1990.

Modern Sources

Charles D. Adams, *Demosthenes and His Influence*. New York: Cooper Square, 1963.

Lesley Adkins and Roy A. Adkins, *Handbook to Life in Ancient Greece*. New York: Facts On File, 1997.

Peter Connolly, *Greece and Rome at War*. London: Greenhill, 1998.

J.F.C. Fuller, *The Generalship of Alexander the Great*. New Brunswick, NJ: Rutgers University Press, 1960.

Michael Grant, *Cleopatra*. New York: Simon & Schuster, 1972.

———, *From Alexander to Cleopatra: The Hellenistic World*.

New York: Charles Scribner's Sons, 1982.

———, *Greek and Roman Historians: Information and Misinformation.* London: Routledge, 1995.

N.G.L. Hammond, *A History of Greece to 322 B.C.* Oxford, England: Clarendon, 1986.

———, *Philip of Macedon.* Baltimore: Johns Hopkins University Press, 1994.

Victor D. Hanson, *The Western Way of War: Infantry Battle in Classical Greece.* New York: Oxford University Press, 1989.

W.G. Hardy, *The Greek and Roman World.* Cambridge, MA: Schenkman, 1962.

Miltiades B. Hatzopoulos and Louisa D. Loukopoulos, *Philip of Macedon.* Athens, Greece: Ekdotike Athenon, 1980.

David Hogarth, *Philip and Alexander of Macedon.* 1897. Reprint: Freeport, NY: Books for the Libraries Press, 1971.

Donald Kagan, *Pericles of Athens and the Birth of Democracy.* New York: Free Press, 1991.

Jack Lindsay, *Cleopatra.* London: Constable, 1970.

A.J. Podlecki, *The Life of Themistocles.* Montreal: McGill-Queen's University Press, 1975.

Jacqueline de Romilly, *A Short History of Greek Literature.* Trans. Lillian Doherty. Chicago: University of Chicago Press, 1985.

Nicholas Sekunda, *Marathon, 490 B.C.: The First Persian Invasion of Greece.* Oxford, England: Osprey, 2002.

Nicholas Sekunda and John Warry, *Alexander the Great: His Armies and Campaigns, 334–323 B.C.* London: Osprey, 1998.

A.M. Snodgrass, *Archaic Greece.* Berkeley and Los Angeles: University of California Press, 1980.

Philip de Souza, *The Greek and Persian Wars, 499–386 B.C.* London: Osprey, 2003.

Chester G. Starr, *The Ancient Greeks.* New York: Oxford University Press, 1971.

———, *A History of the Ancient World.* New York: Oxford University Press, 1991.

A.E. Taylor, *Aristotle.* New York: Dover, 1955.

Rex Warner, *The Greek Philosophers.* New York: New American Library, 1958.

Alfred North Whitehead, *Process and Reality: An Essay in Cosmology.* Ed. D.R. Griffin and D.W. Sherburne. New York: Free Press, 1978.

INDEX

PICTURE CREDITS

ABOUT THE AUTHOR

Historian Don Nardo has written or edited numerous volumes about the ancient Greek world, including *Greek and Roman Sport*, *The Age of Pericles*, *The Parthenon*, *Life in Ancient Athens*, *The Decline and Fall of Ancient Greece*, *The Minoans*, the four-volume *Library of Ancient Greece*, and literary companions to the works of Homer, Euripides, and Sophocles. He resides with his wife, Christine, in Massachusetts.